20 Walks in Wealden

GH00703048

Compiled by Peter Titchmarsh,

in support of Hospice in the Weald

CONTENTS

INTRODUCTORY SECTION

Published by:
White Horse Books

on behalf of:
Hospice in the Weald,
Maidstone Road, Pembury,
Tunbridge Wells,
Kent TN2 4TA
© Hospice in the Weald 2014

First published
1st October 2014
ISBN 0-9526851-8-3

Front Cover Photograph:

The Medway Valley
from Smarts Hill
- the start of our Walk 2

Introducing our area of Wealden Country

The area around the towns of Tunbridge Wells, Tonbridge, Sevenoaks and Edenbridge contains some of the High Weald's loveliest countryside and the aim of this guidebook is to introduce the reader to its many attractive features and to provide a number of walks well away from its busiest corners. The richly-wooded Greensand ridge runs along the northern edge of our area, while the Wealden Country to its south is intersected by the Rivers Eden and Medway. Here is much quiet, rolling farmland, often framed by further woodland - all ideal walking country.

Our Walks Explained

On pages 6-58 we provide details of twenty walks in ascending order of length, from two miles to ten miles. On pages 59-80 our Wealden Country's towns, villages and other places of interest are described in a Gazetteer Section.

We suggest that you start your walks early in the day and return to the starting inn for lunch. In every case you should obtain the permission of the inn's management to park your car and if you are returning for lunch this will normally be obtained. If you are unable to obtain permission we can only suggest that you park at the nearest possible alternative.

Each paragraph of text starts with a reference letter and this cross-refers with the same letter on the accompanying maps. These maps are at a scale of 1:50,000 (about one-and-a-quarter inches to the mile) and are based upon the Ordnance Survey's Landranger series. This guide's area is covered by Landranger Sheets 187 and 188 and by the larger-scale Explorer Sheet 147. The symbols and signs used on the maps are shown in the block at the head of page 4 and there is also a chart below it showing the Landranger and Explorer sheet coverage. If a description of any place passed on the walks is included in the Gazetteer Section it will be printed in **bold**.

Use this book to support Hospice in the Weald Registered Charity No. 280276

While this guidebook's main objective is to offer a series of entertaining walks together with detailed information on our Wealden Country, it is also hoped that it will help to raise funds for Hospice in the Weald (*Registered Charity No. 280276*), whose vitally important work is funded almost entirely by charitable donations. We shall do this by encouraging walkers to raise funds by obtaining sponsorship from friends, relatives and work colleagues, and we shall also ensure that all proceeds on the sale of this guidebook go to the same organisation.

For further details of our fund-raising suggestions please see the inside of the rear cover.

Hospice in the Weald is the leading palliative care provider for the communities of West Kent and northern East Sussex. We are not part of the NHS but are a local charity rooted in the community we serve. We offer varied but integrated services for people with terminal illnesses, and also for their carers and families.

Hospice in the Weald provides specialist palliative care to individuals with terminal or life-limiting illness. This care extends beyond the individual to those important to them, for example, their families, friends and carers. Our care aims to incorporate the individual's physical, psychological, social, religious/spiritual and cultural needs. We therefore provide a multi-professional service to those in need in our community.

Our services include a 17-bed in-patient unit, providing palliative care to terminally ill patients. Our Hospice in the Home service, supports terminally ill patients wishing to stay in their own home. Our Hospice Day Service welcomes over 100 patients with a life-limiting condition every week, providing a range of different experiences and also respite for their carers. Our counselling service affords bereavement counselling for families and carers for as long as they need it and our Lymphedema service offers assessment and treatments to patients requiring palliative care within the Hospice setting.

For more information about our services please visit our web site www.hospiceintheweald.org.uk or call 01892 820 586 and speak to Sara Clark.

The Countryside Code

Be safe: **Plan Ahead** and follow signs. Be prepared for the unexpected. Please respect the working life of the countryside, as our actions can affect people's livelihoods, our heritage, and the safety and welfare of animals and ourselves. Keep to public paths across farmland and walk in single file to minimise path-spread or crop damage. Use gates and stiles to cross fences, hedges and walls. **Leave gates and property as you find them**. **Take your litter home**. Don't forget that litter is not only untidy, but it can also cause great harm to animals and farm machinery. Make sure you don't harm animals, birds, plants or trees. **Keep dogs under close control,** *keeping them on leads when there is any chance of encountering stock. Don't forget that pregnant ewes are very much at risk even from merely playful dogs.* It is your duty to ensure that your dog is not a danger or a nuisance to farm animals, wildlife or other people**.** Take special care on country roads, *usually walk towards oncoming traffic, but on blind bends walk on the outside of the bend where you will be most visible and also wear light coloured clothing.* Make no unnecessary noise. Show consideration for other people and help to make the countryside a pleasant place for all, at home, at work or at leisure.

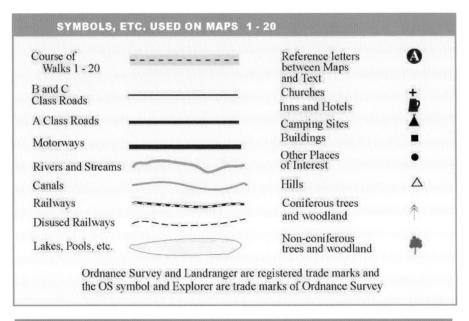

Course of Walks 1 - 20	– – – – – – – – –	Reference letters between Maps and Text	Ⓐ
B and C Class Roads	———————	Churches	+
A Class Roads	———————	Inns and Hotels	
Motorways	———————	Camping Sites	▲
Rivers and Streams		Buildings	■
Canals		Other Places of Interest	●
Railways		Hills	△
Disused Railways		Coniferous trees and woodland	
Lakes, Pools, etc.		Non-coniferous trees and woodland	

Ordnance Survey and Landranger are registered trade marks and the OS symbol and Explorer are trade marks of Ordnance Survey

ORDNANCE SURVEY MAP COVERAGE OF OUR WEALDEN COUNTRY

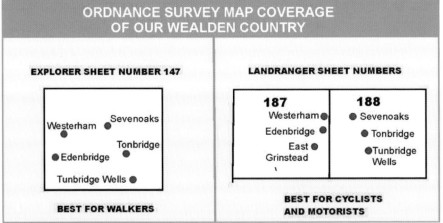

EXPLORER SHEET NUMBER 147

Westerham ●   Sevenoaks ●
●   Tonbridge ●
● Edenbridge
Tunbridge Wells ●

BEST FOR WALKERS

LANDRANGER SHEET NUMBERS

187	**188**
Westerham ●	● Sevenoaks
Edenbridge ●	● Tonbridge
East ● Grinstead	●Tunbridge Wells

BEST FOR CYCLISTS AND MOTORISTS

The preparation of this guidebook has only been possible thanks to the invaluable support of my old friend, Margaret Bates and her daughter, Helen Rahn. Not only have they introduced me to this lovely Wealden Country, but they have also kept a close eye on the wanderings of a walker no longer in his prime! I am also much indebted to my friend, Tony Wilson for all his invaluable help.

Our 20 Walks in Wealden Country

The lengths of these walks are in ascending order, Walk 1 being the shortest and Walk 20 the longest. Length and time details are shown at the head of each walk's starting page.

WALK 1

CROCKHAM HILL - CHARTWELL - CROCKHAM HILL

Memories of Octavia Hill and Sir Winston Churchill

(A) Set out from the Royal Oak Inn, **Crockham Hill** by turning left out of its front door, **crossing the busy B 2026 with great care** and going up right-hand pavement beside the B2026. Pass attractive row of tile-hung cottages on right and turn right just beyond them, down minor road (signed - *Village Hall*). Pass turning on left

> Start from - The Royal Oak Inn, Crockham Hill TN8 6RD
> Tel: 01732 866 335
> Length of walk: 2 miles
> Approximate time: 1¼ hours

to village hall and its car park and then pass school on left. Now pass church, up to left (with its moving effigy of Octavia Hill), and veer right to go through wooden kissing-gate to right of large metal gate. Go straight across sloping field with benches and through small metal gate in cross-fence. Keep in same direction across large field, going over small plank "bridge" crossing line of boggy ground. Now aim downwards for wooden kissing-gate in wooded hedge-line in valley ahead. Through this kissing-gate, over small wooden bridge crossing stream and veer left to go up left-hand edge of field with bushes and stream to left. Near top of field veer left to go over stile and follow up partly-surfaced path between low fences. Path soon becomes stepped and climbs very steeply uphill.

(B) Draw breath at top of steps and go behind back of house before bearing left onto roadway opposite house with oast. Turn left to follow roadway through Mariners Drive (*a private estate, but not indicated as such here*) immediately passing house called

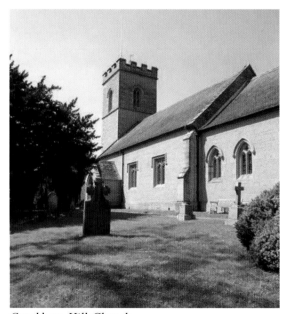
Crockham Hill Church

Springstede on left. Follow road as it climbs gently upwards passing a number of large houses set well back. At end of road cross the bend of a busy minor public road **with very great care**. Veer slightly left to find a signed footpath veering left to initially go parallel with and above the public road. Follow path as it bends to right with hedge to immediate right and start to go gently uphill and then more steeply. At junction of paths with no waymarks turn sharp right to go along the lowest of alternative paths. Soon pass to immediate left of clipped hedge and house, both visible down to right. Path sometimes becomes obscure, but keep in same direction as it starts to gently descend, until reaching track. Now turn right to follow track (part of the **Greensand Way**) as it climbs gently up to a busy minor road. Cross this minor road at bend with **very great care** and bear slightly left to go up bridleway (signed - *Bridleway*) into beautiful woodlands. Bridleway eventually levels out and goes beside wooden fence on right. Pass gated entry to bungalow on right and start to gradually drop down on what is now a footpath. Keep straight ahead at junction of paths (sign - *National Trust Circular Walk*). Keep straight ahead at second junction of paths.

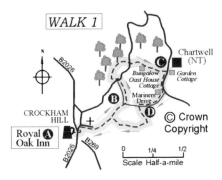

(C) Turn right **with care** onto public road opposite sign of *Garden Cottage*. (*But turn left to go along public road* **with care** *for about half-a-mile before turning right to go into its car park if you wish to visit* **Chartwell**, *once the home of Sir Winston Churchill, now in the care of the National Trust.*) On main route, having turned right, go along public road **with great care walking in single file**. Pass turning to Studio and Lake Cottages on left. Pass Forest Lodge on left. Pass Oast House Cottage on right with post box in wall and 20 paces beyond it turn right up *Mariners Private Drive*, a surfaced roadway (Sign - *Public Footpath*). Pass large and very attractive stone house up to right. Fine views over the Weald to left. Through small wooden gate to left of large wooden gate. Pass various houses, both to left and right.

(D) Turn sharply left down roadway at road junction (sign - *Footpath*) with notice opposite reading *Last Turning Point*. At end of surfaced roadway continue in same direction, to immediate left of small garage, onto soon narrowing path overhung by trees. Follow down this often steep and uneven, partially-stepped path **with great care**. Emerge into open area with charming tile-hung house on left and turn right onto surfaced roadway, dropping down gently. Ignore turning to *Wild Acres* on left and keep on main roadway. Pass house called *Close Farm* on right. Ignore footpath on left to Grange Farm area (NT). Pass small wood on left and almost immediately turn right to go over small stile to right of large metal gate. Go up field to avoid crossing boggy area on left and then turn left to cross it by way of small plank "bridge". (*We crossed this bridge on our outward journey from Crockham Hill.*) Now head for small metal gate in cross-fence and go through it into field below Crockham Hill churchyard with useful benches. At end of field go through small kissing-gate to left of large metal gate and go onto surfaced roadway. Pass

House with oast on Mariners Drive - at point C

turning area for Crockham Hill Church up to right and then school and village hall car park, both also on right. At end of roadway turn left **with care** to walk on pavement beside the busy B2026 passing a terrace of pretty tile-hung cottages on left. Now cross the B2026 **with very great care** and keep down the right-hand pavement to arrive at the Royal Oak Inn thus completing Walk 1 **(A)**.

7

WALK 2

SMARTS HILL AND THE MEDWAY VALLEY

(A) Set out from the Spotted Dog Inn, Smarts Hill by turning left out of its front door and walking down left-hand side of road for about 70 paces. Then turn left just beyond last house on left. Go down steep path **with great care**, soon going over small stile into field. Go down left-hand edge of field with hedge and trees to

> Start from - The Spotted Dog Inn,
> Smarts Hill TN11 8EP
> Tel: 01892 870 253
> Length of walk: 2¾ miles
> Approximate time: 1½ hours

immediate left. Over stile in bottom, left-hand corner of field, down steps and turn left to go along side of busy B2188 **with very great care**. After 45 paces turn right to cross road and go down footpath following finger-post. Go down left-hand side of field with hedge to immediate left. At end of field turn right to go along farm track.

(B) Fork left in farmyard with farm buildings on both sides (this is Nashes Farm, but not indicated here). Pass tall hedge of farmhouse garden on right and small dutch barn on left. Keep on track as it bends gently to right and goes onto straight section overhung with bushes and trees. Pass small pond on right and start to gently rise. At end of track go over stile to left of large metal gate and veer right to go across field following bridleway waymark's direction and following hopefully well-defined pathway. Once over the brow aim for substantial metal footbridge.

(C) Go over footbridge crossing the River Medway and turn right to follow along right-hand edge of field with the Medway just to right. At end of field go over small bridge crossing ditch and curve round to right to follow course of the Medway. Pass through pleasant pasture field with woodlands up to left. Through gap in cross-hedge and keep beside the Medway. Note high-voltage power-line now running parallel to our left. Over small bridge crossing ditch in tree-lined cross-hedge. Keep along field beside the Medway, still to our right. Over stile in cross-hedge using miniature plank "bridge" if muddy. Now veer left temporarily leaving the course of the Medway and aiming well to left of the high-voltage power-line. Go through gap in far left-hand corner of field (no waymark) with winding River Medway again to immediate right. Go straight across next field aiming for small metal gate in wooded cross-hedge. Through this gate and over small plank bridge crossing ditch. Keep along right-hand edge of next field with deep drainage ditch to immediate right (this is not the Medway). Now aim for small metal gate. Through this gate, over small metal bridge and veer to left along short, left-hand side of field and almost immediately turn right to follow its long, left-hand edge. At end of field go over small plank bridge and stile. Keep in same direction across narrow field and go over stile.

Entrance to the Spotted Dog Inn

8

(D) Turn left **with great care** to go along left-hand side of busy B2188. After only 30 paces cross road **with great care** and go over stile. Veer left to go across field aiming for footbridge in hedge. Over footbridge crossing the Medway and turn right to go parallel with right-hand edge of field with the Medway over to right. Go under high-voltage power-line and through small metal gate in cross-fence. Veer slightly right to go across field, going almost due north. On meeting hedge ahead look carefully for small gap near left-hand end of trees above hedge, with wooden bridge just beyond (this may take some finding). Go over this bridge crossing small stream and go up left-hand edge of field with metal fence to immediate left. Pass under large trees near fence-line and drop down at far end of field to go over stile.

(E) Turn right, **with care**, to go along side of minor public road. Almost immediately go straight, not right, at road junction (sign - *Penshurst*). Go steeply up sunken road overhung with trees **with great care**, keeping well into right-hand side and keeping in single file.

(F) Follow road as it bends to right beyond top of hill and then turn left with care to go along track following footpath fingerpost. (*But keep ahead and turn right twice if you wish to make the shortest return to the Spotted Dog Inn at the end of the route.*) Keep along track which soon becomes a narrower path overhung with trees. Keep on path through small wood and turn right onto public road (*but turn left if you wish to visit the Bottle House Inn (Tel: 01892 870 306) - 100 paces along road*). But, having turned right, go beside the public road **with great care**. Bear left at first road junction (sign - *Walters Green*) and almost immediately bear right at second road junction (sign - *Fordcombe*). Soon arrive at the Spotted Dog Inn thus completing Walk 2 **(A)**.

The Medway Valley from the start of Walk 2

WALK 3

GREAT EARLS WOOD AND STAFFHURST WOOD

(A) Set out from the Royal Oak Inn by turning left out of its front door, and going along side of road. After only 25 paces cross road **with great care** to go through wooden kissing-gate beside large metal gate into Great Earls Wood. Note information board on left. Follow gradually narrowing path into wood, soon ignoring small

> Start from - The Royal Oak Inn,
> Staffhurst Wood, Oxted RH8 0RR
> Tel: 01883 722 207
> Length of walk: 3¼ miles
> Approximate time: 2 hours

path branching off to left by small bench on left. Soon fork left following yellow waymark and start to drop down into possibly boggy area before climbing up slope beyond. Go through small gap in cross-fence and keep on boards over another possibly boggy area. Turn right on well-defined track following yellow waymark. Follow track as it eventually curves to left and meets minor public road. Turn left and go along road **with great care** - best to go along right-hand side to face oncoming traffic, but go over to left-hand side where road bends to right. Pass sign on left - *Merle Common.* Pass houses down to left and ignore Public Footpath sign to left. Pass 40 MPH sign on right and after 30 paces ---

(B) --- turn right onto path following Public Footpath sign. Immediately beyond last cottage on left enter wood. Keep up sloping path in wood and watch very carefully for a smaller path forking off to left. Take this left-hand path, which soon runs parallel with the left-hand edge of the wood and passes the back of a house. At end of wood cross busy minor road **with great care**, and go over stile following Public Footpath sign. Veer diagonally right to go across top corner of large field to stile beside large wooden gate. Go over stile into wood and after only 15 paces turn left at junction of paths following waymark indicating - *Self-Guided Trail.* Soon ignore path to right and keep straight ahead. Eventually turn right to go gently upwards, along well-defined track. On reaching waymark pointing right on small wooden fence on right, turn **left** to follow path, now going eastwards. Through narrow gap in small fence across path. Bear right at inverted Y-junction of paths. Bear left onto circular driveway of house over to right (*The Horns*). Follow driveway to reach minor public road and ---

Springtime in Staffhurst Wood

(C) --- turn left to go along this public road **with great care** and immediately beyond Comfort Cottage (on right), turn right to follow Public Footpath sign. Go on narrow path and almost immediately over stile. Keep in same direction along right-hand edge of small field with building to immediate right. Over stile in cross-fence and veer right to go across top, right-hand corner of field (if obstructed by crop, go around right-hand edge).

Go down right-hand edge of field until almost reaching corner, but turn left onto slight track coming in from right-hand gateway. Keep on this track, passing to the immediate left of large pool. Head for cross-hedge well beyond pool but very shortly before reaching it, turn right to locate easily-missed stile. Go over stile and bridge immediately beyond it and keep in same direction across narrow belt of woodland. Go over stile and up across field to immediate right of sporadic line of oak trees. At top of field bear right and keep to right of fenced railway cutting.

(D) Veer right by closed stile on left and follow another sporadic line of oak trees. At end of field go over stile following waymark and keep along left-hand edge of next field. Through small wooden gate in left-hand corner of field and keep in same direction along left-hand edge of next field. On meeting large wooden gate on left go over stile to its immediate right and turn right to go along minor public road **with care.** Pass entry to Caper's Farm on right. Go over bridge crossing the delightfully-named Crooked River. Keep along road ignoring small wooden gate on left just beyond bridge. Turn left to go over stile following Public Footpath sign. Go straight across field aiming for right-hand end of nearest cross-hedge. On reaching end of cross-hedge veer slightly left to go along right-hand edge of next field with sporadic hedge and trees to immediate right, thereby maintaining almost the same direction. At end of field go beneath clump of trees and immediately bear right to go along left-hand edge of this large field with hedge to immediate left, thereby avoiding buildings of Black Robin's Farm which were ahead. At corner of field go over stile beside large wooden gate and through bushy area.

(E) Arrive at public road and turn right to go along it **with great care** for 20 paces. Now turn left to cross road and go onto track into Staffhurst Wood following Public Footpath sign. Follow track as it veers slightly to right and goes up gentle slope. Where large metal gate is visible on edge of wood down to left, veer left off main track and go along well-defined path with edge of wood over to left. Just beyond corner of field over to left turn left onto track by pond on right. Soon fork right at Y-junction of paths and go gently up slope, still on well-defined path. Keep in same direction across open clearing and then veer slightly to right to reach busy public road.

(F) Turn right to go about 15 paces along road and then turn left to cross it **with great care**, and go into woodland following footpath waymark. Veer right to follow minor footpath through narrow belt of trees, first going parallel with road, over to right. Look carefully for stile to left and cross this to go along left-hand edge of small field with wooden fencing to immediate left. Through small wooden gate in cross-hedge and veer right to go diagonally across large field along hopefully well-defined path. Over stile in cross-hedge and go along right-hand edge of next field. Rear of Royal Oak Inn now visible ahead. Turn left in first corner of field and soon turn right at second corner keeping to left of both hedge-lines. Over stile to right of large metal gate and turn right, **with care**, to go beside busy public road. Almost immediately arrive at the front door of the Royal Oak Inn, thus completing Walk 3 **(A).**

WALK 4

SHIPBOURNE - IGHTHAM MOTE - SHIPBOURNE

(A) Set out from the Chaser Inn, Shipbourne by turning left out of its front door, ignoring turn to its car park up to left and its garden beyond, and then turning left up roadway towards church, following Greensand Way fingerpost. Go through lychgate into churchyard and go on path to right of church, soon passing its north porch. Through stone-bordered

> Start from - The Chaser Inn, Shipbourne TN11 9PE
> Tel: 01732 810 360
> Length of walk: 3½ miles
> Approximate time: 2 hours

kissing-gate and go straight ahead on path with hedge to immediate right. Through gap at end of small field and keep in same direction to go across centre of large, gently rising field (*could be very muddy after rain*).

Well before end of field go over stile to enter wood and keep in same direction following a well-defined path. At intersection of paths and tracks in wood fork left, up rise. At top of rise keep straight on, ignoring cleared ride to right.

(B) Soon bear right and go over stile before

Our path just beyond Point B

turning right to go along minor public road. (*Budd's Oast, a private house, just off route along to left.*) After 25 paces turn left, off road and go over stile with Ightham Mote Estate (NT) signed. Bear right to go through wide gap before turning left to go up left-hand edge of field with hedge to immediate left. Near end of hedge on left veer right to follow well-defined path across remaining corner of field. At end of field bear left to go over small plank bridge and continue in same direction up hill with scrubby triangular section of field to left. Path now becomes steeper and soon has hedge to its immediate left. Through gap in cross-hedge at end of field and up next field, climbing all the way. Fine views back towards Shipbourne - church may just be visible. Through wooden kissing-gate and veer left to follow waymark's direction, going up left-hand side of field, aiming just to left of house below wooded Wilmot Hill, visible up ahead.

(C) At top of field go through wooden kissing-gate and turn right onto track in front of house. *We have now joined the course of the* **Greensand Way** *and we shall follow this all the way back to Shipbourne.* Keep straight on at inverted Y-junction of tracks following Greensand Way waymark. Veer left just beyond barns and oast houses on right, keeping on main track.

(D) Pass barns of Bridlepath Farm on right and turn right onto surfaced public road. Good view of **Ightham Mote** (NT) immediately ahead at this point. Bear right keeping on road (*but if you wish to visit Ightham Mote, turn left to go down tree-shaded driveway and at bottom turn right when Ightham Mote comes into view. Now go parallel to Ightham Mote and go beyond it, up slope, before turning left into National Trust staff car park. Bear left beyond car park and then right, following sign, "Entrance" to arrive at Visitor Reception).* Back on main route,

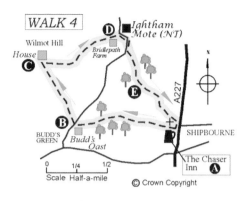

keep on road passing farm buildings on right and as it starts to descend bear left to go over stile (Greensand Way waymark) and go down right-hand side of field with hedge to immediate right. Through gap at bottom of field and up left-hand side of next field. Over stile in top left-hand corner and into wood. Keep on well-defined path up through wood and then gently down again, with fences on both sides of its latter course. Over stile at end of wood - a possible glimpse of Shipbourne church ahead left, above treetops. Go down field with fence to immediate left and bear left near bottom to go along broad swathe of field with fence to left and woodland to right.

(E) At end of field cross farm track and go over stile before immediately veering right to go across small grassy area. At its end, go along fenced path with wood to left. Go over two stiles beyond end of fenced path and go along left-hand edge of field with wooded hedge to immediate left. Cross surfaced driveway and keep along field edge with Shipbourne church soon coming into view. Cross second surfaced driveway aiming for stile just to right of church. Over stile and immediately turn left to go through the stone-bordered kissing-gate that we went through on our outward journey. Go along path through churchyard passing north porch on right. *If visiting church please use boot scraper provided.* Now leave churchyard through lychgate, go down short roadway and turn right to return to the Chaser Inn, thus completing Walk 4 **(A)**.

Ightham Mote

WALK 5

IDE HILL - THE WOODMAN INN - HANGING BANK - IDE HILL

Note - After wet weather the short, steep descent beyond Point D should only be tackled by experienced walkers.

Start from - The Cock Inn, Ide Hill TN14 6JN
Tel: 01732 750 310
Length of walk: 3½ miles
Approximate time: 2¼ hours

(A) Set out from the Cock Inn, Ide Hill, by turning left out of its front door and go along small road below and to left of grassy bank, following sign - *Camberwell Lane*. Soon bear left at inverted Y-junction and follow road as it slopes downwards, with houses on both sides. At end of road bear left to go around edge of small green overhung with trees. Just beyond green go through small wooden gate with concrete footpath sign just visible on ground beside it and below a telephone pole. Go down grassy path and through kissing-gate below tree. Go diagonally right across centre of large field, following hopefully defined path in a due north direction. Fine open views ahead. At end of field go through kissing-gate, cross concrete road and immediately turn right onto driveway following footpath sign, with house called *The Ramblers* on left. Almost immediately bear slightly left to go along path to left of *Cordons Farm* sign with house to left and fencing to right. Soon bear left to go between hedge to left and fence to right. Cross driveway and go through wooden kissing-gate with wooden barn to left. Go straight across centre of field, keeping almost due north. At far right-hand corner of field go over small stile below bushy tree at right-hand end of cross-fence. Keep in same direction with hedge to left and wooden fence to right. Over stile and keep along left-hand edge of field and over next stile in left-hand end of cross-fence.

(B) Over yet another stile and turn right **with care** to go along narrow public road opposite entrance to *Little Norman Fields*. Keep on road down hill, pass cottage on right and *Brook Place Farm* on right. Immediately beyond house called *Shipley* on left, turn left, off road following concrete *Public Footpath* sign and go up track. On emerging into field turn right to go diagonally up across large, sloping field following hopefully well[-defined path. Go onto track at entry to Willow Wood (*not indicated*) and

The Woodman Inn - just beyond Point C

almost immediately turn right at X-rds of tracks onto wide track. Bluebells much in evidence here in late spring and early summer. Ignore track coming in from right and then fork right near top of rise keeping on wider track. Through kissing-gate and turn left **with care** to go along public road overshadowed by trees. Woodlands soon on both sides of road. Fork right keeping on road to right of large triangular green. After about 70 paces beyond end of green turn left following footpath sign and go up driveway to immediate left of house. Immediately beyond garage bear right off driveway to go through gap onto path with hedges on both sides.

(C) Beyond building on right turn left with **very great care** onto busy B2042. Keep on left-hand side of road for a few yards and then cross to the other side **also with very great care**. Pass the Woodman Inn on right - *Tel: 01732 750 296 - possibly stopping for refreshments!* Just beyond inn take the first of two paths indicated to the right by going along very short, less well-surfaced track and over stile to left of large metal gate. Go

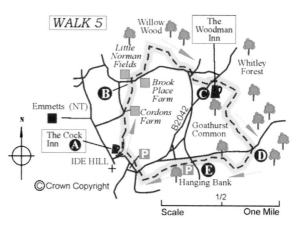

across middle of field on hopefully well-defined path and at its end enter wood on track soon veering slightly right to go over small stile and then veering left to go down track beyond. Small field to left, with woodands everywhere else. Turn right at T-junction of tracks soon dropping down into valley. Bear left to go over X-rds in valley and keep on track as it climbs out of it. Over another X-rds of tracks and still climbing but near end of small field over to left branch to right, off track and go steeply up small bank onto waymarked path. **Watch for this with care.** Follow path through woods with care, as it is not too well defined.

(D) Eventually drop down and turn right **with great care** onto public road and after only about ten paces turn left off road onto wide track following footpath sign. Track eventually becomes a path and bears left with fine views through trees over to the right. Path now starts to drop down very steeply. **If this steep path is muddy be very careful.** At bottom end of wood turn right to join more level footpath and go through small metal gate. Now turn right to walk along right-hand, upper side of large sloping field. We have now joined **The Greensand Way**), follow Greensand Way waymarks for the rest of this route. Splendid open views to left including **Bough Beech Reservoir**. Veer up to right of field and go over small stile. Keep on path along bottom edge of wood with fence to immediate left, but where path starts to turn away from the edge of wood fork right and go steeply up hillside - path stepped at one point. Eventually bear left and follow more level path, with traffic noise indicating that we are now parallel with a road to our right. Pass bench on left with fine view through gap in trees. This area is known as Hanging Bank, with steep slopes down to our left all the way along here.

(E) Emerge from wood, cross minor public road **with care** and go straight across the small Hanging Bank Car Park. Go onto bridleway to immediate right of Hanging Bank Information Board, still on **Greensand Way**. Almost immediately veer right to keep on main track. Fork right at next Y-junction and keep straight on at top of slope. Eventually drop down to turn sharp left at inverted Y-junction. Start to drop gently down and turn sharp right to join house's driveway. Keep along driveway serving several houses. Bear left onto very busy B2042 and cross it **with great care** before continuing along path on its right-hand side. Almost immediately bear right onto quieter road (sign - *Ide Hill*). Pass rear of village shop etc. on left and keep up hill ignoring road to left just beyond. Arrive at Ide Hill village green on left and the Cock Inn on right thus completing Walk 5 **(A)**.

15

WALK 6

IDE HILL - TOYS HILL - EMMETTS GARDEN - IDE HILL

(A) Set out from the Cock Inn, **Ide Hill**, by turning right out of its front door and going along road with great care with village green to left. Turn right at roundabout into Sundridge Road and immediately turn left to go along minor road with school on right. At end of this short road go through kissing-gate to left

> Start from - The Cock Inn,
> Ide Hill TN14 6JN
> Tel: 01732 750 310
> Length of walk: 3½ miles
> Approximate time: 2¼ hours

of large metal gate following Greensand Way waymark. (We shall now follow the waymarked **Greensand Way** until reaching Point C - the car park at **Toys Hill**.) Keep along left-hand edge of large field soon dropping down steeply. In bottom left-hand corner of field, ignore kissing-gate to left and go through gateway ahead. Keep down left-hand edge of next field and at its end go through kissing-gate to left of large metal gate. Keep down steep track along left-hand edge of field and, where hedge turns to left, keep straight across rest of field aiming for small gate on edge of wood ahead.

(B) Through this small metal gate and over bridge crossing stream in narrow belt of woodland. (From here we have a long climb, only ending at Toys Hill.) Go up across field heading just to right of nearest wood. On reaching wooded, top edge of field, veer left to follow field edge. Soon reach a very welcome memorial bench, from which there are outstanding views over the Weald to the long line of Ashdown Forest on the distant horizon. After ten paces beyond bench turn right to go through squeeze-stile into **Toys Hill** Wood. Climb up path into wood and soon ignore path to right. At intersection of paths bear left to go up slope and go round wooden barrier. At next intersection of paths, turn second left. Bear right and cross public road **with great care** to arrive at **Toys Hill** Car Park.

(C) *(Note: There are a number of woodland paths starting from here. These are waymarked with different coloured arrows and described in National Trust leaflets usually available from*

a dispenser over to the right of car park.) Keep along left-hand edge of car park and go straight into wood on wide path to the immediate left of signboard. Soon bear down right and then go upwards. Bear left at junction of paths following red waymark and bear right to go up slope. Now pass the site of **Weardale Manor**, with its splendid views westwards, interesting signboard and small monument

Our path just beyond Ide Hill

to two brothers killed in the First World War. Keep in same direction beyond the Manor site, still on the Red Route. Go straight, not right, at junction of paths keeping on Red Route. Fork right at next junction of paths onto narrower path by small wooden bench, leaving the Red Route. Go around wooden barrier across path, now following Green Route into coppiced woodland. Bear slightly right, then left and then turn

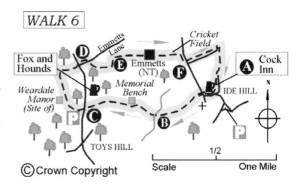

right by post with green waymark (Yes, you are still on the Green Route!). Pass waymarked post and now on both the Green and Red Routes. Follow path as it veers to right and then left to drop down to public road T-junction. *(Turn right here and go along road **with great care** for about 250 paces if you wish to visit the Fox and Hounds Inn (Tel: 01732 750 328).*

(D) Cross road at this T-junction **with great care** into Emmetts Lane, but immediately fork left on path into wood - still on Red Route. Follow path into wood as it veers right to go parallel with Emmetts Lane. Soon bear right and cross Emmetts Lane **with great care**. Go on path into wood - still on Red Route. Go around wooden barrier and drop downwards on partly-stepped path. Soon rise again and on meeting next waymark post, turn left off Red Route onto smaller path, almost immediately going around wooden barrier. Soon dropping gently downwards passing post with bridleway waymark and therefore now on bridleway. Bear left onto wider, winding track and follow it, soon going upwards.

(E) At top of slope, turn right at crossing of tracks and follow sign *Ram Pump Walk*. Go through gap beside stile following sign *Ram Pump Walk*. Pass entry sign to Emmetts Garden. Please pay at Reception if visiting the garden, but otherwise please walk through on the right-of-way, although this is not signed. Enter **Emmetts Garden** and keep on wide surfaced path, first passing to the immediate right of tearoom. If you are passing straight through, keep on this path, ignoring turnings to right and left and heading towards single poplar tree. Eventually bear right by large, white gate on left and start long, straight descent beyond Emmetts Garden (Sign - *Public Footpath*). Through small wooden gate beside large wooden gate. Pass small cart-shed over to right. Pass welcome bench on left, overlooking beautifully-maintained cricket field.

(F) Through small wooden gate to left of large wooden gate and turn right to go along right-hand side of public road **with great care**. Turn left at road junction onto minor public road (signed - *Norman Street*). Go along this quiet but very narrow lane with high banks, **so please take care**. Ignore small metal gate in thick hedge to right. Where road bends to left by house called *The Ramblers*, veer right and right again to go through metal kissing-gate (signed - *Public Footpath*). Go straight across centre of large field soon aiming just to left of house between two trees. Through metal kissing-gate to left of house and enter **Ide Hill**. Through small wooden gate and veer right to go to right of "island" with trees. Keep along side of road with houses on both sides. Eventually bear right and keep right to arrive at the Cock Inn on right, thus completing Walk 6 **(A)**.

WALK 7

EDENBRIDGE - EDEN VALLEY - HAXTED - EDENBRIDGE

(A) Set out from the Eden Valley Museum, Edenbridge, by going northwards along the left-hand side of the High Street. Pass Lloyds Bank on left and after 15 paces turn left to go along path on left-hand side of smaller road. Turn left at traffic lights to go beside the busy relief road of St Aignan Way (but not signed as

> Start from - The Eden Valley Museum,
> 72, High Street, Edenbridge TN8 5NR
> Tel: 01732 868 102
> Length of walk: 4 miles
> Approximate time: 2 hours

such here). Keep along left-hand pavement, soon passing supermarket on left. Immediately beyond supermarket car park turn right **with great care** to cross St Aignan Way via traffic island. On reaching far side of road veer left to go down short, surfaced path. At bottom of path turn right to go along narrow strip of meadowland with trees and bushes to left and houses visible to right. At end of narrow strip veer slightly right to go through wide gap with trees to left and housing estate fence to right. Beyond gap turn left to go beside trees, now on left and single pole on right. After 25 paces beyond pole go down steep little bank and then along left-hand edge of field with tree-shaded and old, largely-obscured mill race to immediate left.

The River Eden beyond Point B

(B) Over bridge in left-hand corner of field with River Eden now visible down to left. Keep in same direction through small plantation ignoring path forking to right (*which we shall use on our return journey*). Go over small bridge with 39-45 War pill-box on right. Keep close to left-hand edge of field and veer right with River Eden now visible to immediate left. *No clear sign of medieval moat which is just to our right near here.* Pass large tree on left and keep on track as it enters woodland, still keeping parallel with the River Eden. Keep on track as it emerges from wood with tree-lined river still to left. Go through gap in left-hand end of cross-hedge and keep on well-defined path with tree-shaded river still to left.

(C) Over small wooden bridge and through complex L-shaped metal barrier, observing notice - *Caution - Aeroplanes - Footpath crosses* , *taxiway and airstrip.* **Take care, this facility is still in use by light aircraft**. Now head cautiously across this large field in a south-westerly direction to reach narrow gap in tree-lined hedge (not easily identified). Through gap in hedge to cross bridge with waymark and go straight across right-hand side of small field. At its end go onto tree-lined track with woods on both sides. Pass large pool on left as we emerge from wood, keeping on broad track. Where track turns left, go straight ahead, over stile to left of large wooden gate. Keep in same direction across centre of field and at its end go over small bridge at intersection of footpaths. Keep in same direction across small field, with Cernes Farm just visible over to right.

(D) At end of field turn right onto farm drive and well before reaching Cernes Farm turn left off drive. Go over small wooden bridge and through metal kissing-gate.

Immediately turn right to go along right-hand edge of field, soon following a public footpath sign. Keep just to right of low-voltage power-pole with farm buildings over to right. Through sporadic hedge- and tree-line and keep along right-hand edge of field, following direction of power-line. Through another gap in sporadic hedge-line and keep in same direction with hedge to right veering away from us. Over plank bridge and stile well to left of metal gate, following *Tandridge Border Path* waymark. Keep in same direction

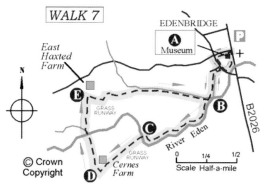

across centre of next field, still closely parallel with power-line. At end of field keep to left of power-pole and over substantial bridge crossing River Eden. Keep in same direction across narrow section of large field and over another substantial bridge crossing another branch of the River Eden. Bear slightly left to follow path along left-hand edge of field with bushy trees to left. Pass another warning sign regarding aircraft - **take this seriously as our path crosses another airstrip**. Follow path as it enters bushes and pass small pool on right. Path now starts to bend to right and to gently climb with bushes on both sides. Veer right onto wider track with buildings of East Haxted Farm ahead.

(E) Turn right onto track with some trees on its left and East Haxted farmhouse up to left and fine views over to right. Pass yet another sign warning about aircraft - **take this seriously**. Cross grassy aircraft taxiway. At top corner of field go through gap and turn left to go over plank bridge and up along left-hand edge of field with trees to left. At top of field turn right to go along track across field with fine views to left and right. At end of field go through wide gap and initially keep in same direction before veering left near bottom of field and going through gap in bottom left-hand corner. Go through metal structure in this gap and keep on track along left-hand edge of next field. Veer very slightly right to go over X-rds of tracks and keep on track along left-hand edge of field with drainage ditch to immediate left. Through wide gap in cross-hedge into next field and keep along its left-hand edge. Ignore gap with bridge beyond to left and go straight ahead through large gap in cross-hedge into wooded area following well-used path. Playing fields just visible over to left.

(B1) Bear left onto wider path (*re-joining our outward route*) and over bridge. Now go up right-hand edge of playing fields with old mill race in bushes to right. At top end of playing fields go up steep little bank with trees still to immediate right. Keep in same direction, heading towards houses but after 40 paces turn right to go along narrow strip of meadowland with houses visible to left and trees and bushes to right. Where strip of meadowland veers to right, turn left to go up short, surfaced path. At top of path turn right and, **with great care**, cross the busy St Aignan Way via traffic island. Once across, turn right and immediate veer left off main pavement to go down narrower path. Follow this path beside the River Eden and veer left before reaching bridge to go up path. Turn left and go along the left-hand side of Edenbridge High Street. Pass timbered buildings to left, and the King and Queen Inn on right. Pass small road up to church on right, pass the Old Crown Inn on left, with its signboard over the centre of the street, and arrive at the Eden Valley Museum on left, thus completing Walk 7 **(A).**

WALK 8

STONE STREET - GODDEN GREEN - STONE STREET

(A) Set out from the Padwell Arms, Stone Street by going straight across the road from its front door and bearing diagonally left down a surfaced track by 30 MPH sign. This is a right-of-way although its sign may be obscured by hedge growth. Pass house on right and soon emerge into more open country with hedge to left and field to right. At top of gentle rise, by gate just

Start from - The Padwell Arms, Stone Street TN15 0LQ
Tel: 01732 761 532
Length of walk: 4 miles
Approximate time: 2¼ hours

before reaching road, turn very sharp right to go diagonally across field along wide avenue bordered by young (*in 2013*) trees. At end of avenue keep in same direction onto narrow path with bushy hedge to right and fence to left.

The Padwell Arms - at the start of our Walk 8

(B) Over stile, cross minor public road **with care** and go down roadway opposite (signed - *Public Bridleway*). Almost immediately pass house on right and then a second house on right, with oasts visible over to right, just beyond. Keep down narrower track, soon bearing right at junction of paths. Track soon becomes overhung by trees. Keep on track where the beautiful

Great Roger's Wood commences on right. Still keep in same direction before bending to left and going up gentle rise and then bending to right. Now drop down into valley and go steeply up again into another wood. Pass house and garage on right. Keep on now semi-surfaced driveway soon ignoring two footpaths to left. Pass *Damson Mead* - a large house on right. Pass another large house on right with pretty lantern on its roof. Pass entry to the Cygnet Hospital on right. Now on to better surfaced roadway. '

(C) Bear right **with great care** at inverted Y-junction on to busier road in Godden Green and walk along right-hand side of road. Pass wide village green on right, with duck pond on left and the Buck's Head Inn (*Tel: 01732 761 330*) on left just beyond. Keep on road up gentle rise and after 80 paces, turn right, off road following footpath fingerpost and forking left to aim for wooden fence in front of garage. Go onto path to immediate right of this wooden fence and below horse-chestnut tree. Go down narrow path and soon emerge into more open area following defined path through sparse woodland following waymark on post. Pass sign stating *Caution Flying Golf Balls* and soon veer well to right to go across golf course aiming well to right of golfers' green marked by flag. Search carefully before entering woodland for point indicated by waymark on post. Veer slightly right here to follow well-defined path through wooded area and cross small track. Pass another *Caution Flying Golf Balls* sign and keep on path with woodland to left and golf course's fairway parallel to right. Immediately beyond golfers' tee on right, turn right following waymark's direction, cross narrow roadway and go along broad track into woodland.

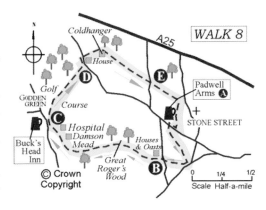

(D) Go through gap beside large metal gate and veer left to go along left-hand side of public road **with great care**. Immediately beyond house on right, turn right, off road and go up path following bridleway fingerpost. This sunken path immediately starts to go upwards and there follows a long climb up through woodlands. At top of path turn right onto surfaced roadway signed *Bridleway*. Well before reaching wooden gate signed *Coldhanger*, fork left off roadway onto track into woods (*not waymarked at time of writing*). Soon pass house over to right with tile-hung garage just beyond. Now on a long path running along a wooded ridge with the land sloping away to the right. If the main path is very muddy it may be preferable to use stretches of a less-well-defined path running parallel to its right - the choice is yours. Keep straight on ignoring unsigned path to left.

(E) Cross minor public road **with great care** and keep in same direction following bridleway fingerpost and ignoring footpath waymarked track down to right. Now continue in same direction along ridge path. Just before reaching next road, where **Stone Street Church** is visible a short distance ahead, turn down right finally leaving bridleway and following footpath waymark. Follow defined path steeply down through woodland. Halfway down slope, go straight ahead ignoring path to right by waymark post. Path narrows with fence to right and sporadic hedge to left. Pass large house on right and at end of path keep in same direction down surfaced driveway with wrought-iron gates to *Stone House* up to right. Turn right **with great care** on to public road and keep along its right-hand edge. Pass house on left and almost immediately turn right to return to the Padwell Arms, thus completing Walk 8 **(A)**.

Duckpond at Godden Green

21

WALK 9

UNDERRIVER - ONE TREE HILL - BUDD'S GREEN - UNDERRIVER

(A) Set out from the White Rock Inn, Underriver by turning right out of its front door and going northwards along public road **with great care**. Pass attractive village sign on left. Pass stile on right, which we shall use on our return journey. Now starting to climb upwards and soon fork left by brick barn on left onto roadway (signed -

Start from - The White Rock Inn,
Underriver TN15 0SB
Tel: 01732 833 112
Length of walk: 4¼ miles
Approximate time: 2½ hours

Bridleway). Pass sign on left - *Kettleshill Cottage*. At end of roadway go onto path with house called *Black Charles* on right. Keep up path overhung with trees, climbing steadily all the way. Just before reaching roadway, turn right (sign - *Restricted Byway*). Now keep up sunken, and often muddy pathway overhung by trees - still climbing. On reaching gate on right veer left and then right to keep in approximately the same direction up path, partially stepped at this point.

(B) At top of this long and very steep path (*at Carters Hill, but not indicated here*) turn right just beyond metal gate following *Greensand Way* waymark. *We shall now follow the* **Greensand Way** *until Point* **C**. Now on narrow path with bluebell woods to left and field to right, with splendid views beyond it. Watch out for tree roots. Eventually pass wooden fencing on right and then attractive garden on right. Veer left by white gate on right and **with great care** veer left to go up beside public road. Immediately pass Carters Hill House on right and soon bear right, off road, onto wide path following *Greensand Way* finger post. Keep on path up through wood. Ignore path coming in from left - this comes from the One Tree Hill Car Park. Pass through open space with bench to left, from which there are splendid views southwards out over the Weald - this is part of the National Trust's One Tree Hill area. Leave this area, taking the lower of the two paths following *Greensand Way* waymark. Pass small wooden bench on left and almost immediately turn right following *Greensand Way* waymark passing wire fence on left for a few paces before going over low stile, leaving National Trust's One Tree Hill area. Path now narrower and soon starting to drop down steeply. At bottom of slope turn right onto surfaced driveway by Rooks Hill Cottage's gates. Go steeply down driveway passing large wooden gate on left before turning left through metal kissing-gate following *Greensand Way* fingerpost. Now pass field with farm buildings

on right and with woods still on left. Through wooden kissing-gate with National Trust sign *Ightham Mote*. Keep on path as it gets narrower with field now on right. Ignore path to left keeping straight on. At end of field on right turn sharp right and go steeply down short, partly stepped path. At bottom of steps turn left to follow track. Pass brick-built well-head on left. Emerge onto driveway with house ahead left, and ---

A welcome rest at One Tree Hill

(C) Turn right to go through wooden kissing-gate leaving the Greensand Way and go down field on slightly defined pathway. Through wooden kissing-gate and go down right-hand edge of next field but taking care to avoid boggy area part way down. Through gap at bottom of field and keep along edge of next field with wood on immediate right. Follow path as it veers away from wood. Over small wooden bridge in hedge gap and veer right in next field. Follow defined path cutting across large

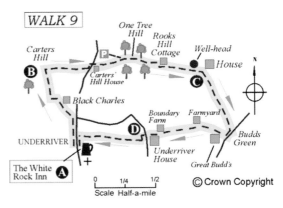

right-hand corner of field and then keep to immediate left of hedge up the rest of the field. At end of field veer right and go over stile beside large wooden gates and turn right to go along public road **with great care**. Soon enter Budd's Green hamlet with wide green on right. At end of green turn right (sign - *Restricted Byway*) and veer right off driveway to Great Budd's just before its entrance gateway. Keep on path to immediate right of fence with view of fine house to left, with barn just beyond. Follow path in woodlands with large pond over to left. Over stile to left of large metal gate and follow track across park-like field. Follow track as it bends to left passing through sporadic hedge-line. Go straight across next large field leaving track which bends away to left. At end of field go over small wooden bridge and over two stiles through narrow belt of woodland. Keep straight across field following waymark's direction. Over stile beside large metal gate and go across lower end of farmyard with buildings up to right. Over stile beside large wooden gate and over another stile immediately beyond. Keep along right-hand edge of field with wood to immediate right. Large house with tall chimneys visible ahead. Over stile in top, right-hand corner of field and bear right keeping on path on edge of woodland. Tall garden wall visible over to left and keep in same direction heading for large wooden gate and on reaching it turn sharp left to go up track. Pass Duck's Grove, a weather-boarded house (possibly a converted barn) on right. Keep in same direction across surfaced area and down surfaced roadway passing Boundary Farm, a house on right with brick wall beyond it. Pass small terrace of cottages on right and ---

(D) Turn left **with great care** onto public road. Pass pond on right and entrance gates to Underriver House on left. Now turn right, off road, and go over stile and small wooden bridge. Go straight across park-like field following fingerpost's direction. Good view back to handsome Underriver House. Over stile beside large metal gate and initially keep up left-hand side of field with short line of poplar trees on left. Beyond trees keep in same direction straight across field aiming just to right of pair of oak trees. Go over stile just to right of oak trees and keep in same direction across next field. Over small 'bridge' crossing ditch in middle of field and keep in same direction beyond it. Go over stile in wire fence and keep in same direction across field, going down slope before going over stile beside metal gate. Keep in same direction along left-hand edge of next field aiming to the immediate right of poplar trees. Over stile to left of large metal gates and down short, narrow path before going over second stile. Now turn left along public road **with great care**. Now entering Underriver passing house called *The Forge* on left and *30 MPH* sign beyond. Soon arrive at the White Rock Inn on left, thus completing Walk 9 **(A)**.

23

WALK 10

FOUR ELMS - BOUGH BEECH RESERVOIR - FOUR ELMS

(A) Set out from the Four Elms Inn, at **Four Elms**. Turn left out of the inn's front door and cross the busy B2027 **with great care**. Go along footpath, soon crossing not very apparent stream and re-cross road **with great care**. Go through metal kissing-gate below tree and keep along left-hand edge of field with stream

Start from - The Four Elms Inn, Four Elms, Edenbridge TN8 6NE
Tel: 01732 700 460
Length of walk: 4½ miles
Approximate time: 2¼ hours

down to left. Four Elms Church, with its slender spire, visible over to right. At end of field go over small plank bridge and keep along left-hand edge of next field with stream still down to left. At end of field go over stile and veer slightly right to go across centre of next field, soon aiming to left of cart-shed. If possible go over small stile well to left of large metal gate, but if difficult, go through gate ensuring that it is left as found (open or closed). Keep in same direction across next field aiming for right-hand end of re-entrant hedge coming in from left. Over stile where hedge meets post and wire fence and turn left to follow round left-hand edge of very large field. Bear right keeping along edge of field. Now passing wood on left as path starts to climb up bank.

(B) At top left-hand corner of field go through kissing-gate, cross public road **with great care** and bear slightly left to go over stile. Go diagonally across small field aiming for small stile in wooden cross-fence - this may be difficult to locate. Go over this stile and keep in same direction across broad ride and go over small stile in second wooden cross-fence. Veer slightly right passing through two sporadic hedgelines beneath trees.

Our path well beyond Little Chittenden

Keep down small field beyond, aiming for left-hand end of cross-hedge. Go through , wooden kissing-gate and bear left passing tree-shaded pond down to right. Almost immediately go left through metal squeeze-stile. Now turn right to go **with very great care** along right-hand edge of the very busy B2042. **Go in single-file and keep well into the side**. Pleasant woodlands on both sides of the road. Pass house on right with barn - *Little Chittenden*. Follow road as it bends to left and passes roadway to right and almost immediately bear right up a narrow pathway with hedge to left and trees to right. Turn left to go over stile into field and turn right to keep in same direction, now along right-hand edge of field. At end of field bear left and after 25 paces turn right to go over stile and into woodlands. Soon cross plank bridge and turn left to go over stile and keep in same direction down right-hand edge of field with woodland still to right. Follow path as it bends to right and then left, as it emerges into field. Turn left and follow gently down narrow field with trees and bushes to left - this could be boggy after wet weather. Over small bridge crossing stream and keep on up grassy track with woods to left and field to right. Through large metal gate, over public road with great care and go down track to immediate right of tile-hung house - *Piggott's Cottage*. Through gap to right of large metal gate and continue along track. Over stile beside large metal gate and keep in same direction on track

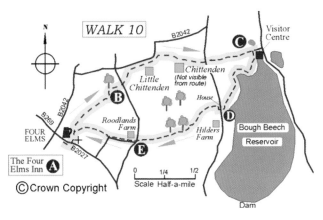

across centre of large field. Through large metal gate at end of track and go down left-hand side of large field. Oast of the **Bough Beech Visitor Centre** visible ahead. At bottom of field, through wooden kissing-gate and go ahead before turning right to arrive at the **Bough Beech** Visitor Centre.

(C) Having visited the Centre, with its interesting displays, its hop garden and its hide overlooking a modest wetland pond, go back through our original access - the wooden kissing-gate and turn left to go along the bottom, left-hand edge of field. At corner of field go through wooden kissing-gate and follow well-used path through plantation. Pass small bench on right. At end of plantation go through wooden kissing-gate and straight across narrow field. Over small plank bridge and turn right through wooden kissing gate. Go up path within right-hand edge of wood (primroses here in late spring). Follow path as it bends down to left and soon pass glimpses of **Bough Beech Reservoir** to left. Pass benches to right and soon turn right through wooden kissing-gate (sign - *End of Nature Trail*). Follow hopefully well-defined path up across field

Bough Beech Reservoir from our path

aiming just to right of power-pole. On reaching power-pole veer slightly left and go down across next field aiming just to left of house and garden. Partial view of **Bough Beech Reservoir** ahead left. At end of field go over small stile to left of house and garden and along narrow path with tall hedges on both sides. Turn right to follow this path between fences.

25

(D) Turn right **with care** to go along public road, and after about 70 paces, turn left to go through metal kissing-gate. Now go along right-hand edge of field with hedge to immediate right and Hilders Farm visible over to left. At end of field turn right to go through small metal gate and then left to keep in same direction as previously, going along left-hand edge of large

Barns at Roodlands Farm

field. Pass between two water-troughs. Near end of field turn left to go through small metal gate and turn right to keep in same direction by going along right-hand edge of field. On reaching oak tree on right turn left to go across field keeping to left of small parallel stream. At end of field turn right to go over bridge crossing stream and after ten paces turn left to go over stile. Now turn right and follow up right-hand edge of large field soon starting to pass woodlands on right. Keep on gently rising track along right-hand edge of next large field. At end of field keep in same direction across wide grassy space soon passing twin power-poles on right and into next field. Keep along right-hand edge of field but where hedge starts to veer to left turn right through gap to immediate left of small stile. Go carefully down steep and often muddy slope **with great care** and veer left to go along minor public road.

The Four Elms Inn, Four Elms

(E) Bear right at Y-junction just beyond Roodlands Farmhouse on right. Pass *Little Blackmoor* - house on left and Roodlands Farm barns on right. Keep down road, but where it turns sharply to left, go straight ahead through kissing-gate to right of large metal gate. Bear right on track and where it soon arrives at large metal gate, turn left to go along right-hand edge of field with hedge on immediate right. At end of field go over stile to right of large metal gate and pass over possibly boggy area. Keep along right-hand edge of next field with hedge to immediate right. At end of field keep along short and possibly muddy track to emerge into next field. Now go diagonally across this field aiming for left-hand corner - Four Elms Church now visible over to left. In corner of field go over small plank bridge and go along right-hand edge of next field with stream down to right. At end of field go through kissing-gate, cross the busy B2027 **with great care** and turn right to go along footpath beside road. Soon re-cross road to arrive at the Four Elms Inn, thus completing Walk 10 **(A)**.

WALK 11

HEVER - HILL HOATH - MARKBEECH - HEVER

> Note: Some sections of this route could be very muddy. We suggest that it is best walked in the summer months.

> Start from - The King Henry VIII Inn, Hever TN8 7NH
> Tel: 01732 862 457
> Length of walk: 5 miles
> Approximate time: 2½ hours

(A) Set out from the King Henry VIII Inn, Hever, crossing busy road **with care** to go through lych-gate into churchyard, joining the course of **The Eden Valley Walk**. Keep down path passing church porch on our left. Bear right at bottom of churchyard and then bear left to go over bridge in woodlands. Keep on narrow path with field soon to right and then parallel with estate road to left. Soon bend to right ignoring small gap to left. Keep on woodland path with fences on both sides and estate road still to left. Now climb quite steeply and go over large wooden bridge crossing now sunken estate road. Path now widens as it continues to climb. Eventually merge with estate road and follow this along outside, right-hand edge of woods with fields over to right. Go through gap to left of large metal gate across estate road.

(B) Pass two houses on right and immediately beyond second house fork right, off road, onto narrow fenced path. Pass old wooden shed on left and path is overhung with bushes beyond this. Through gap to right of gate and cross minor public road **with care**. Go through kissing-gate and down fenced path with woods to right and field to left. At end of field turn right to go over stile. Woods now on left and field on right. After turning left, go over small wooden bridge crossing stream and follow steep, partially-stepped path as it climbs up into woods. Veer slightly right, then left **to cross grassy ride with care as this may be used for horse galloping**. Re-enter woods and through kissing-gate to keep on wide path which continues to climb gently, with fence not far to left. Bear left at inverted Y-junction with fields now on right and woods to left. Path now sunken with rocky sides and is for this reason known locally as *Hoath Canyon*. Gradually drop down beyond the "canyon" and ---

(C) --- at intersection of tracks just before reaching Hill Hoath hamlet, turn right to go across open space and through kissing-gate to left of large metal gate. Initially go along left-hand edge of very long field but soon veer away from this edge and head across field, keeping to left of first bushy clump and to right of second

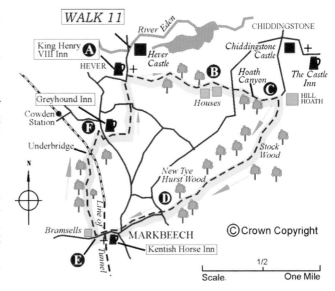

27

bushy clump. Now head for top, right-hand corner of field to locate kissing-gate. Immediately beyond kissing-gate, turn left to go along path with fences on both sides. Veer slightly left to follow path into Stock Wood (*which is signed*). Ignore small path to left and keep straight ahead up wider path. Ignore waymarked path to left and keep straight on, up slope, keeping in same general direction. Now, just within left-hand edge of wood with fields visible to left. At end of Stock Wood go through gap to right of large metal gate and veer left to go along right-hand edge of field. Keep in same direction, straight across field and go on to track to immediate right of large rhododendron bushes. Veer left to go on wide track into woods with open field soon to right. Where track bends to right by large oak trees, go straight ahead on path with fence to immediate left, soon passing field on left. Re-enter woodlands going through gap to right of large metal gate to enter New Tye Hurst Wood (*which is signed*). Keep in same direction, soon ignoring track to left. Follow our track as it rises gently for most of its length and is likely to be very muddy in all but the driest of months.

Markbeech Church

(D) Through gap to left of large metal gate and, **with great care**, keep straight ahead at road junction to go beside public road (sign - *Markbeech*). Pass Markbeech entry sign on left and pass first house on right - *High Buckhurst*. Over offset X-rds with the Kentish Horse Inn (*Tel: 01342 850 493*) on left (sign - **Edenbridge**). Pass church on left, leaving Markbeech on the Cowden Pound Road. Pass Village Hall on right and soon ignore driveway down to right. Keep well out of Markbeech.

(E) Turn right, down fingerpost-signed footpath immediately before gateway and garden fence to *Bramsells* (very modestly signed). Go along narrow path with fences on both sides. Fine views ahead over the Eden Valley to the Greensand ridge. Pass concrete farmyard on left and keep down sunken path on left-hand edge of field. This path is uneven and often very muddy - **take special care**. Ignore small wooden gate to right and follow path into woodland, soon veering right to join wider track through further pleasant woodlands. Track eventually narrows to a small path and after some distance it then veers right to go under high railway embankment. Now veer gently to left keeping on track through wood. Pass buildings on right and ---

(F) --- turn sharp right to go up beside public road **with great care**. Soon cross road to the Greyhound Inn (*Tel: 01732 862 221*) and **immediately** beyond the far end of ' the inn building, locate difficult-to-spot, small wooden gate. Go through this gate and along narrow, tree-shaded pathway with fences on both sides. Pass pond on left and post-and-rail fencing to right. At junction of paths turn left to go over stile and initially keep across right-hand side of field before veering right, down into wooded area, keeping in approximately the same direction. Pass pond on left and keep along right-hand edge of next field. Locate kissing-gate below trees down to right before reaching far, right-hand corner of field. Through kissing-gate and go carefully down through wooded area. Turn left on to public road **with care**. Go along road and where it bends to left, bear right, off it, to go along wide path with woods on right, following footpath fingerpost. Enter Hever village, passing school on right and the King Henry VIII Inn straight ahead, thus completing Walk 11 **(A).**

WALK 12

WESTERHAM - CHARTWELL - WESTERHAM

(A) Set out from the King's Arms Hotel in the centre of **Westerham**, by turning right out of its front door and going along pavement beside the very busy A25. Note the statues of General Wolfe and Sir Winston Churchill on the large sloping green over to left, Pass bus stop on left and after 45 paces pass entry to Water Lane (*from which we shall emerge near the end of our walk*). Keep down the rather narrow pavement beside the A25 with care. Pass the Old Vicarage on right and ---

> Start from - The King's Arms
> Hotel, Westerham TN16 1AN
> Tel: 01959 562 990
> Length of walk: 5 miles
> Approximate time: 2¾ hours

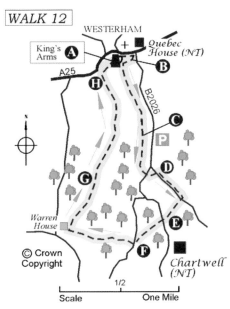

(B) --- turn right into little Mill Street where **Quebec House** (NT) comes into view ahead, over to the left of the A25. Go to the end of Mill Street and bear right across parking area to go up path into wooded area and soon through kissing-gate following footpath waymark. Bear right across corner of field before going over footbridge crossing stream. Keep on well-used path along right-hand edge of field and through gap in cross-hedge. Now turn left to go up left-hand edge of large, steeply sloping field following footpath waymark. Ignore small stile to left and keep along edge of field before going over stile in left-hand end of cross-fence. Keep in same direction, going parallel with the left-hand edge of next field. Fine views back to the long line of the North Downs. Keep in same direction passing waymark post in field well to right of its edge. Go down steep slope near end of field now keeping to its left-hand edge.

(C) In bottom, left-hand corner of field turn left to go through metal kissing-gate and follow well-defined path into woodland. Keep on path as it bends to right and rises gently. Fork left at Y-junction of paths following footpath waymarks. Keep straight on at next path junction ignoring turning to left. At intersection of paths turn left and almost immediately right before crossing short boardwalk (*footpath waymark*), thereby keeping in approximately the same direction. Now on left-hand side of stream-bed, going almost exactly southwards and climbing gradually. On reaching busy minor road cross it **with great care** and go onto path into woodland (*footpath waymark*). Ignore unsigned cross-path and keep in same direction as previously.

(D) Soon turn right to go beside quieter minor road **with great care**. After about 600 paces turn right, off the road and immediately take the **left-hand** fork to follow footpath waymark into wood - now on the **Greensand Way**, but this may not be signed as such here. Veer left when meeting wooden fence and go along narrow path with wooden fence to right and post-and-rail fence to left. Watch out carefully for projecting tree roots.

29

(E) At end of path, cross busy minor road **with great care** and go up steps into wood following Public Footpath sign (*but turn left and left again if you wish to visit* **Chartwell,** *the home of Sir Winston Churchill, by walking through its large car park*). On main route, continue up steep path into wood. We are still on the **Greensand Way**. Fork right at Y-junction of paths (signed - *Greensand Way*) and soon take a further right-fork (signed - *Greensand Way*). Keep straight on (signed - *Greensand Way*) ignoring path to right. Cross track and after ten paces bear slightly right (signed - *Greensand Way*). After 50 paces, on meeting wooden fence ahead, turn right to go beside wooden fence. Where fence turns left, keep straight down steep path, which could be slippery after rain.

(F) At bottom of path bear slightly right to cross busy minor road **with great care** and go down track (signed - *Bridleway*). Keep down roughly-surfaced track, soon passing entry gate to *April Cottage* on left. Bear left to follow track up into wood and soon ignore paths to left and then to right, thereby keeping up main path (signed - *Greensand Way*). Ignore further paths to left and right and go straight up slope (signed - *Greensand Way*). Pass dark, timbered house on left (modestly signed - *Warren House*), and opposite it, turn right, away from its grassy parking area and into wood. Cross two woodland tracks following footpath waymark (we have now left the Greensand Way). Keep in the same northerly direction, soon forking left at path-junction and into young plantation (*defined paths may still be obscured by tree-clearance and replanting operations*). Now start to drop down quite steeply and head down towards sight of open field beyond wood.

A rest in the garden at Chartwell

(G) Arrive at small stile on edge of wood and cross it into very large field. Bear left to go along field on slight terrace which veers to right to follow its left-hand edge with wood up to left. Pass just to left of waymarked stile and keep along left-hand edge of field. Near end of field go over stile to left of large metal gate to go onto track beyond it following *Footpath* waymark. After 80 paces turn right to go down track (waymarked - *W4*). After 30 paces turn left to go over stile in fence and go down track just to left of fence. Now in very long valley field which curves attractively with woodland to right and bank with a few trees on it, above to left. At end of field go over stile beside large wooden gate onto track with fence to left and bushes and trees to right.

(H) Pass house on left and almost immediately turn right to go over bridge (sign - *Greensand Way*) and kissing-gate beyond. Keep along lower, left-hand edge of sloping field. Soon start to watch carefully for small wooden kissing-gate in hedge down to left. When located, turn left to go through this gate (sign - *Greensand Way*) onto narrow path with wooden fencing on both sides. Over stone stile and keep up narrow path with walls soon on both sides - this is known as *Water Lane*. Now in **Westerham** as we emerge onto pavement beside the very busy A25 with its wide, sloping green on the far side. Note the statue of General Wolfe almost opposite and that of Sir Winston Churchill well over to the right. Turn left to go on pavement beside the A25. Just beyond top of slope, arrive at the King's Arms Hotel, thus completing Walk 12 **(A)**.

WALK 13

COWDEN - CRIPPENDEN - WAYSTRODE - COWDEN

(A) Set out from the Fountain Inn, Cowden, by turning left, out of its front door and turning left again to go up beside street. Bear right at top of slope and pass attractive houses both on left and right of High Street. Almost immediately turn left into North Street. (*But go straight ahead if you wish to visit the church.*) Ignore turning on

> Start from - The Fountain Inn,
> Cowden TN8 7JG
> Tel: 01342 850 528
> Length of walk: 5¼ miles
> Approximate time: 2¾ hours

left to Chanters Mead and keep straight up North Street. Ignore entries to Chestnut Place on left and to Prior's Way on right. Ignore footpath sign at entry to Little Priors on right. Follow North Street as it bends to left and becomes Spode Lane.

(B) Just before reaching small barn on left, turn right through offset gates following public footpath fingerpost. Go across field veering slightly to left, following well-defined path and aiming for low-voltage power-pole in bushy hedge. Veer left to go through wide gap into next field. Veer slightly left to go across next field heading for wide gap in bushy hedge ahead - still on well-used path. Go through this wide gap and keep in same direction across next field heading for large metal gate.

(C) Go over stile to left of metal gate and cross public road **with great care**. Go over opposite stile following public footpath fingerpost. Keep in same direction across field still following well-used path. Cross concrete roadway and follow track as it enters wood, bending left. Bear right onto concrete roadway passing barns of Ravenscroft Farm on left. Pass entry gate to bungalow on right and veer right onto grassy track beyond. Now keep along right-hand edge of field with wood to immediate right. At right-hand corner of field go along path through narrow belt of woodland and soon emerge into field. Turn left to go along left-hand edge of field with wood to left. Soon turn left onto driveway crossing bridge. Keep up wide drive of Leighton Manor Farm beneath avenue of trees.

(D) At junction of driveways keep straight ahead down slope following footpath waymark. (*At about this point our route is crossed by the course of the **Roman Road** that ran from London to Lewes, but there are no signs of it here.*) Where roadway bends down to left, turn right to go down bank keeping in same direction as previously, to head for waymark post on edge of wood (this post could be hard to spot). Go down steps just to left of post and over footbridge. Up very slippery slope beyond bridge - take **great care here**. Go through wooden kissing-gate and straight across field following waymark direction and aiming for wooden gate ahead. Go through this wooden kissing-gate to right of metal gate and go straight across next field following waymark direction. Go through wooden kissing-gate to left of large metal gate and veer left to go down large field to left of large oak tree. Lovely rolling, wooded country ahead. Aim for wooden gate as way ahead becomes visible and start to drop steeply down into

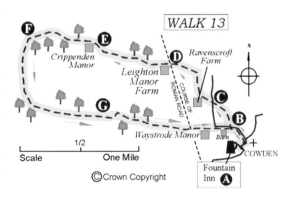

31

The Fountain Inn, Cowden

valley bottom. Go through wooden kissing-gate and keep straight into woodland following waymark direction. Almost immediately veer right to follow track, going uphill in wood. Watch carefully for waymark post on right and turn left here following waymark direction. Soon go over small footbridge **with great care** and over stile just beyond. Initially keep up left-hand edge of field but soon veer right to aim to right of lovely mellow-brick Crippenden Manor with its stout chimneys and 17th-century origins.

(E) Go through small metal gate to left of large metal gate in fence well to right of manor and go across farmyard. Keep in same direction across drive and veer slightly right and then left onto track to immediate right of ornamental pond. Veer left beyond pond to go down track with wooden fencing on both sides and garden over to left. Through large metal gate following blue bridleway waymark and head across field keeping just to right of two oak trees. In left-hand corner of field go through large metal gate onto track in wood. Bear left at far edge of wood and follow pleasant grassy track with wood to left and fence to right. Ignore small metal gate on right and keep on grassy track, which is a bridleway. Keep on bridleway as it turns to the right and starts to climb, with wood still on left.

(F) At intersection of tracks watch carefully for metal kissing-gate on left and go through this into a short section of woodland. (*We have now joined* **the Sussex Border Path** *and shall remain on it for the rest of the walk to Cowden. However this path does not appear to be signed as such at any point.*) Follow path as it winds through wood and at its end go through kissing-gate into field. Turn right to go along right-hand edge of field with hedge to immediate right. Turn left in corner of field and go along its right-hand edge with a wood on right. (*You may wish to cut across this corner but we are following the right-of-way.*) Ignore large metal gate on right and continue following right-hand edge of field. Before reaching corner of field, where hedge starts to veer left, go over stile beside large metal gate. Keep down left-hand edge of field with woodland to left and turn left

Gateway beyond Point F

to go over stile to left of large metal gate. Turn right to go down right-hand edge of field with wood to right. At bottom right-hand corner of field go over stile to left of large metal gate following footpath waymark. Go onto track through woodland belt and soon emerge into field. Keep along left-hand edge of this field with woods to left. Now dropping gently downwards with woods still to left. Turn left in left-hand corner of field and go onto track in wood following footpath

Our path heading down towards Cowden

waymark. Follow track as it bends to left and then to right, with footpath waymark on post on left.

(G) Emerge into large field and go diagonally right across centre of this field on slightly-defined footpath following waymark direction and heading for slight gap in trees and bushes ahead. At end of field go through gap in bushes and veer slightly left to go across next, much smaller field following hopefully defined path. Veer slightly right to drop gently down and go onto path into wood. Watch for this with care. Over footbridge crossing stream and follow path carefully as it climbs up through woodland. This path could be very slippery after rain. (*At about this point our route is once again crossed by the course of the* **Roman Road** *that ran from London to Lewes, but, as previously, there are no obvious signs here.*) Turn right at T-junction of paths following footpath waymark and eventually go up steps. At end of wood go through wooden gate and keep straight ahead across lawn with pond to left. Now in the grounds of Waystrode Manor, which lies over to right, but is not visible from our route. Keep in same direction along driveway with trees and hedge to right and lawn to left. Soon pass entry gate to Waystrode Manor on right (but not signed as such). Keep along drive passing pond on left and walk around to right of cattle-grid with great care. Keep straight on to join public road and walk along this **with great care** passing houses on left and right.

(B1) Pass small barn on right and ignore footpath sign to left, just beyond. (*This is common with Point* **(B)** *and we shall now follow our outward route back into Cowden*). Enter Cowden on Spode Lane and bear right into North Street. Keep down to the end of North Street before turning right into High Street. Soon bend down to left to arrive at the Fountain Inn thus completing Walk 13 **(A)**.

High Street, Cowden

WALK 14

LEIGH - CHARCOTT - LEIGH

Start from - The Fleur de Lis Inn,
Leigh TN11 8RL
Tel: 01732 832 235
Length of walk: 5¼ miles
Approximate time: 2¾ hours

(A) Set out from the Fleur de Lis Inn, Leigh by turning left out of its front door and immediately cross minor road coming in from left **with very great care**. Now go along pavement beside the very busy B2021 (sign - Penshurst). (*Be prepared to endure the noise of busy traffic for the next ten minutes - there is no alternative!*) Pass the long estate wall of Hall Place on right and an impressive lodge also on right. Pass many houses on left and a garden supply company also on left. Soon after road Y-junction ahead is signed and another entrance gate to Hall Place is opposite, cross the B2021 **with very great care**. Now go along the very narrow verge on the right-hand side of the B2021 **with very great care, going in single-file**.

(B) Thankfully soon turn right, off the roadside verge and onto concrete roadway following footpath fingerpost. Pass houses on left and enter Prices Wood (not signed here), keeping on roadway. At end of wood on left turn left off roadway following footpath waymark and go along left-hand edge of large field with Prices Wood to immediate left. (*We shall now follow the irregular northern edge of Prices Wood and Black Hoath Wood until reaching a minor road at* **(C)**, *but detailed route directions are still included.*) Where edge of wood turns to left, keep straight across narrow section of field and turn right at waymark post on wood's edge ahead. Now go along left-hand edge of field with wood on immediate left. Pass trees over to right and turn left at corner of wood and follow along left-hand edge of this very large field with wood still to left. Turn right in next corner of field and go along its left-hand edge with wood still on left. About 100 paces short of gap in cross-hedge ahead, turn left into wood following footpath waymark (**watch for this with care**) and go over minute plank-bridge. Follow defined path through projecting section of wood to go over small footbridge and emerge into field. Bear left to go along left-hand edge of field with wood still to our left. Now going gently upwards with fine open views over to right. Veer left to continue following edge of wood joining short track.

(C) Turn right **with care** onto minor public road and go along it. Turn left **with care** at T-junction (sign - *Charcott*). Soon enter hamlet of Charcott and turn right beyond first houses on right (sign - *Charcott*). Follow road as it bears round to left by small triangular green. Pass the Greyhound Inn on right (*Tel: 01892 870 275*) and soon turn right at T-junction onto farm drive following footpath fingerpost and sign - *Charcott Farmhouse B & B*). Soon fork right to go through small metal gate beside large metal gate following footpath

The Greyhound Inn, Charcott

34

fingerpost. Go diagonally across field with farmhouse visible over to left. Pass to left of tree and clump of bushes and go though kissing-gate to right of old metal gate. Keep in same direction along left-hand edge of field with hedge to immediate left. Cut across left-hand corner of field and

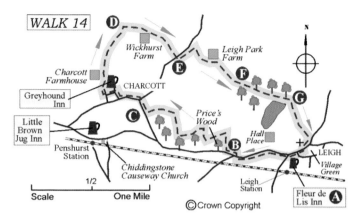

dip down to go through gap in trees beyond. Keep in same direction across centre of next large field and at its end keep along right-hand side of now parallel hedgeline.

(D) At end of field go through gap in hedge and immediately turn right at intersection of paths following footpath waymark. Go down right-hand edge of field with hedge and trees to immediate right. At bottom of field go through gap (or gate) in cross-hedge and keep in same direction up right-hand edge of next field with hedge and trees to immediate right. At end of field go through small metal gate to right of large one and turn left on to farm road. Follow road as it bends to left. Pass substantial Wickhurst farmhouse on right, smaller house on left. Bear left joining better-surfaced farm road and pass house with oasts on right. Keep straight down long surfaced road with fine open views ahead. Pass houses on both sides of road and at T-junction immediately beyond them ---

(E) --- go straight across minor public road **with great care** to go through kissing-gate and over small bridge following footpath fingerpost. Turn left to go along left-hand edge of field with hedge and trees to immediate left. Hedge is replaced by fence before corner is reached. In left-hand corner of field go through small metal gate and turn

right onto concrete farm road. Follow road as it bends to left and then to right. Pass pond on left with Leigh Park Farmhouse partially visible beyond it. Turn right by oast houses on left to go through small metal gate to left of large metal gate. Go down left-hand edge of field and in its corner go through small metal gate and across footbridge.

Leigh Park Farm

35

Go up left-hand edge of next field with hedge to left and at top of field go through large metal gate (*ensure that this is left as found - either open or closed*). Keep along left-hand edge of next field until reaching wood on left.

(F) Go through squeeze-stile into large wood. Follow reasonably well defined path,

Path through the churchyard, Leigh

which soon becomes wider with parallel fence over to its left. Through gap in cross-fence, still in wood, and now on narrow path with fences on both sides and risk of partial obstruction by bush and tree growth. Field visible to right, but wood still on left and fences still on both sides. Wood now again on both sides.

(G) Through tall kissing-gate at end of wood and turn right at junction of paths. Now go along right-hand edge of large park-like field with fence to immediate right. This must have been part of Hall Place's park. Through metal kissing-gate in cross-fence and keep along right-hand edge of next field with fence still to immediate right. At end of field go through metal kissing-gate onto narrow path, soon passing impressive entrance gate to Hall Place on right as we enter Leigh. Immediately beyond gate and lodge turn right to go through lych-gate into churchyard. Keep along path to left of church passing well to left of its south porch. Turn left through gate and down surfaced road. At bottom go across the busy B2027 **with very great care** and turn right to go along pavement beside road - Leigh's High Street. (But turn left if you wish to

visit Leigh's large and beautiful village green with cricket field.) Continue along the left-hand side of the B2027, soon passing Post Office Shop, neat row of cottages and a further shop. Pass the old village water-pump under its shelter and finally arrive at the Fleur de Lis Inn, thus completing Walk 14. **(A)**

Leigh village green overlooked by its church

WALK 15

MARKBEECH - COWDEN - MARKBEECH

(A) Set out from the Kentish Horse Inn, **Markbeech** by turning right out of its front door and head out of village on minor road. Near end of village pass *Hilary Cottage* on right and keep on road as it gently drops down. Bear right at road junction by houses on left (sign - *Cowden Station*). This is Horseshoe Green, but is not signed as such. Pass driveway to *Edells* on right.

> Start from - The Kentish Horse Inn,
> Markbeech TN8 5NT
> Tel: 01342 850 493
> Length of walk: 5½ miles
> Approximate time: 3 hours

(B) Pass Horseshoe Cottage on left and after 40 paces beyond it, turn left to go over stile. Veer left to go up field aiming well to left of belt of woodlands on brow. Now drop down towards left-hand end of hedgeline and go through gap into small wooded area, veering right to follow waymark's direction. Soon go over stile and keep in same direction across centre of sloping field, soon aiming to left of low-voltage power-pole. Veer left beyond power-pole to go along wooded hedgeline on left-hand edge of field, soon passing waymark on post below large tree. Go 70 paces beyond this post, turn left to go over small stile in hedge and veer right to go up across field aiming to right of trough in field and waymarked post beyond, in field. Keep in same direction beyond post to locate stile at edge of wood below. Go over stile into woodlands and follow path along and within its lower left-hand edge. In May this wood is beautifully enriched with bluebells. Over stile at end of wood and emerge into long field. Initially aim just to left of first clump of trees and beyond this ---

(C) --- veer right to go into first gap in trees to right and follow up increasingly clear signs of track. Go over rudimentary "stile" to left of metal gate and go up track that becomes muddy and sunken as it continues upwards. No waymarks here. Soon emerge into field and go across it approximately south-eastwards, aiming for left-hand end of woodlands projecting from the right. Once over the brow keep along right-hand edge of field which curves round to the right. At far corner of field pass water-trough and go over rudimentary "stile" to left of large metal gate. No waymarks here. Go left down sunken track which curves to left before emerging from trees into right-hand edge of large sloping field, with pile of large rocks probably still on left. Keep down this track with rocky "cliff-face" up to right.

(D) At end of track go over difficult stile to right of large metal gate and keep in same direction to go **with care** down into valley on minor public road. Pass attractive tile-hung house on right with timbered gable-end and barns beyond. Ignore footpath sign to left. Over bridge crossing small stream. Ignore second footpath sign to left and over small bridge with low brick parapet.

The Kentish Horse Inn, Markbeech

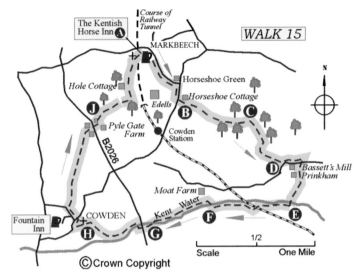

WALK 15

After 30 paces turn right, off road , to go up surfaced drive overhung by trees. On reaching gate across drive with house called *Prinkham* just beyond, veer left to go through small metal gate to right of large one. Go on grassy track across paddock with house visible to right and go to immediate left of wooden shed through probably boggy area. Through small metal gate into next field and turn right to go down field before veering left to follow its lower, right-hand edge. Soon veer right to go over stile beneath bushes and keep along right-hand side of next field aiming for squeeze stile and bridge.

(E) Go over this bridge crossing the Kent Water stream and turn right to go along right-hand edge of field with Kent Water over to right. (*We have now crossed from Kent into Sussex and will be following the Sussex Border Path, although at the time of writing this does not appear to be waymarked as such. The county boundary follows the Kent Water, a small tributary stream flowing eastwards to join the Medway. We shall now follow its upstream course westwards for about one and- a-half miles .*) Over stile below trees and keep along right-hand side of next field following its curving edge. Where path and river go sharply to right, go straight ahead across projection of field. Soon bear left to go up track under railway bridge. Through large metal gate and turn right following fingerpost. Go along right-hand edge of field with fence and wood to immediate right. At end of field go over stile and veer right to go parallel with right-hand edge of next field keeping in same direction. Over bridge into wooded area and over yet another bridge with the Kent Water very close to right. Eventually emerge into field and turn right to follow its wooded right-hand edge. Towards end of field bear right into woodland and turn left at X-rds of paths with large bridge to right.

(F) Bear left, not crossing this bridge, and after only seven paces, turn right to go over second bridge crossing the Kent Water and through small wooden gate. (*We are now on the north side of the Kent Water, back in the county of Kent.*) Go along left-hand edge of large

Bluebells in woodland just before Point C

Looking down our track to Point D

sloping field with Moat Farm visible up to right. Through small wooden gate at left-hand end of cross-fence and keep on left-hand edge of next field. Through another small wooden gate in cross-fence and keep along left-hand edge of next field. Near end of field turn left to go over large wooden bridge re-crossing the Kent Water and back into Sussex. Turn right to go over stile and go along right-hand edge of field with the Kent Water to immediate right. Through gap or over stile and keep along small, narrow field to left of the Kent Water. Over another stile or through gap and then over yet another stile to go along grassy pathway. Over another stile and turn right **with great care** to go beside the busy B2026.

(G) After 50 paces cross road **with very great care** by the *Welcome to Kent* sign and, having crossed the Kent Water, leave road through large metal gate to go along left-hand edge of field with tree-shaded Kent Water now on left. (*We are now back in Kent once again.*) Cut off small corner of field aiming for large wooden gate and then over stile to its right. Keep along right-hand edge of small field with hedge to immediate right. Veer right to cross a track with wooden gate to right and initially keep just to left of hedge. Soon veer left to go through large wooden gate and go up left-hand edge of field with woodlands to immediate left. At top, left-hand corner of field go over stile into wooded area. Follow path down into woodland and soon turn right on more clearly-defined track and onto grassy ride with woods on both sides. This soon opens out into wider field and drops into valley. Now keep along left-hand edge of field and bear left to go over bridge crossing stream. Go up right-hand edge of field with hedge to immediate right. Spire of **Cowden** church soon visible ahead right.

(H) Over stile at entry to **Cowden** with new cemetery on left. Bear slightly right to enter churchyard and pass church on right. Pass south porch and west door before leaving

Cowden Church

39

churchyard. Cross road to go along village street, first passing house called *The Forge* on left. Turn right into North Street (*but go straight ahead and soon turn left if you wish to visit the Fountain Inn - Tel: 01892 770 213*). Ignore turnings to left and right, but immediately before North Street bends to left, turn right onto driveway for *Little Priors* and immediately go through wooden kissing-gate on right. Now turn left to follow around left-hand edge of field. Watch carefully for gap in hedge on left and go over stile. Immediately bear right around drive with house to right and go through gap below yew tree onto tree-shaded path. Go along left-hand edge of field soon veering right onto track with trees to left and hedge to right. Bear right at intersection of paths, veering away from woodlands now on left. Fork right by waymark post, now dropping gently down right-hand edge of next field, with trees to immediate right. Keep down into valley to right-hand corner of field to go through gap in fencing to left of large entry on right. Over bridge crossing small tree-shaded stream. Head straight up large field, initially aiming for left-hand edge of woodlands projecting from right. Now go up hill, out of valley and aim for large gap in cross-hedge on skyline. At top of field go over stile in its left-hand corner well to left of gap with large metal gate. Go along top, right-hand edge of field having changed direction from northwards to westwards. Follow round edge of field to immediate left of farm buildings. Now watch carefully for small stile on right. Go over this stile into farmyard. Go through metal gate, veer left and soon through metal gate to meet the B2026.

(J) Now veer slightly right to go across the busy B2026 **with great care.** Go into less rural farmyard of Pyle Gate Farm with barn on right and house on left. Keep straight down track passing house with attractive garden on left. Veer left on track and soon bend to right to follow down hill along very pleasant, tree-shaded track. Pass entry drive to *The Grove* on left and start to climb gently upwards - still on track. Turn left at junction of tracks beneath massive beech tree. On reaching small building ahead fork right, off track onto pathway - view of lovely, tile-hung Hole Cottage over to left. Keep along attractive woodland path ignoring large metal gate on right. Over stile and go up left-hand edge of field. At top of field go over stile on left and immediately turn right, thus keeping in same direction. Keep along right-hand edge of this large field and at end of hedgeline on right turn right to keep on right-hand edge of field. **Markbeech** church now visible ahead left. Bear left on to track by gateway on right and now heading direct for church. Turn right to go over stile into **Markbeech** churchyard and go on path keeping to right of church. At end of churchyard turn right to go on drive to car park of the Kentish Horse Inn, thus completing Walk 15 **(A).**

Markbeech Church - from our final stile

WALK 16

GODDEN GREEN - ONE TREE HILL - KNOLE - GODDEN GREEN

(A) Set out from the Buck's Head Inn, **Godden Green**, by turning right, onto the road and passing duckpond on right. Immediately fork left onto minor road. Keep up hill passing entrance to The White House on left. Pass entry to Cygnet Hospital on left and go onto roughly surfaced roadway. Pass house on left with attractive lantern on its roof and start to go gently downhill before passing entrance to Damson Mead on left.

> Start from - The Buck's Head Inn,
> Godden Green TN15 0JJ
> Tel: 01732 761 330
> Length of walk: 5½ miles
> Approximate time: 3 hours

(B) Where roadway starts to bend to left, turn right, off roadway onto public footpath. Keep on path up into woods with wooden fence to right and then chain-link fence to right. Over crossing of paths in wood and soon ignore path coming in from left. Now ignore track bending away to right and keep ahead on footpath. Edge of wood only a few paces to our left but we keep within wood, parallel with this edge. At end of wood go over stile and keep in same direction across large field keeping just to right of short, sporadic tree-line. At end of field go over stile with small building probably just visible beyond it. Turn left immediately beyond stile to go down surfaced roadway. Pass house on right and fork left by large tree beyond it onto grassy track. Through small wooden gate to left of large metal gate and immediately turn right onto well-defined track just before entering farmyard. Soon on semi-surfaced driveway passing Lower Fawke Farmhouse on left.

(C) Turn left onto surfaced public road by Fawke Farm-house on right. Keep downhill on road but where road bends sharply to the left, bear right off road onto signed track into wood, ignoring footpath signed up to its left. Keep in same general direction climbing gently and eventually, at top of rise, veer right joining wider path

The Buck's Head Inn, Godden Green

coming in from left. Arrive at intersection of paths by National Trust sign *One Tree Hill*. Keep in same direction, just to left of National Trust sign, going across wide track. Keep on path uphill with wooden fencing to left. Go under possible bar across track and follow wider track, still gently rising. Cross open area beyond wood and climb steep little bank. Go ahead for a few paces to arrive at bench from which there are splendid views out over the Weald.

41

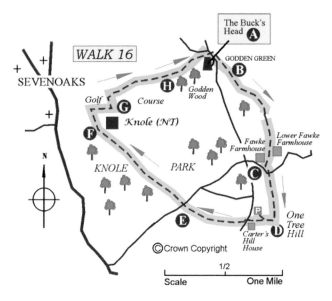

(D) Now turn right, down onto well-used path into woods (this is part of the **Greensand Way**, but possibly not waymarked as such at this point). Soon keep in same direction following Greensand Way waymark and ignoring path to right, *unless you wish to take this path to head for car park, which is a short distance ahead.* On main route, now starting to descend more steeply. Turn left onto public road and go down it **with great care**. Immediately beyond Carter's Hill House on left, veer right, off road and almost immediately turn right onto path to immediate right of large white gate - still on Greensand Way. Follow path between fences as it starts to rise. Bluebells in woods up to right, splendid views over to left. Veer right onto track and almost immediately veer left to go over stile beside small metal gate. Now go diagonally across horse paddock following between thin, yellow-painted marker posts. At end of field go over stile and into woodland.

(E) Cross public road **with great care** and go through tall kissing-gate in deer fence, entering the great Knole Park and keeping on the Greensand Way. *Please take care when encountering the deer who graze freely in the park. Although they might appear tame, please don't feed them.* Keep in same direction following well-used path. Cross avenue with surfaced drive (this is the Chestnut Walk, but not signed as such here). Now following a surfaced drive - still on the Greensand Way. At the top of a gentle rise veer slightly right off surfaced drive and almost immediately cross another surfaced drive (at the end of another avenue). Now follow a grassy path aiming just to the left of the large outer wall of Knole's garden coming in from the right. On meeting corner of wall keep

A glimpse of Knole from our path approaching Point F

Our pathway through Knole Park beyond Point G

in same direction and go beside it' to its immediate left, still following the Greensand Way. Glimpses of **Knole** through ornamental gates in wall.

(F) At next corner of wall veer right following Greensand Way waymark to go diagonally across open area with Knole's entrance tower over to right. (*But if you wish to visit Knole turn right to walk directly to entrance gate below tower.*) Pass just to right of the small, partly-concealed roof of Knole's brick-domed ice house. Bear left just beyond the ice house, down narrow surfaced path and on meeting waymark post on right in valley bottom, turn right, leaving Greensand Way and follow *Explore Kent* waymark onto driveway. Ignore waymark post on left and follow driveway, taking a left fork, signed *Car Park*. Keep up driveway over brow of hill with good view of Knole now well over to right. Start to drop downwards and over crossroads. Go down driveway into valley.

(G) Turn left in valley and go along track in avenue of trees. At end of avenue veer right keeping on track passing notice-board on right stating **Beware of golfers playing from left**. Now briefly cross golf course and keep on track as it rises gently out of valley. Through tall kissing-gate to right of large wooden gate, leaving Knole Park and entering left-hand edge of Godden Wood. Keep in same direction dropping gently downwards on track in wood.

(H) Immediately beyond lowest point of track, fork right onto path in wood following sign *Godden Green ¼ mile*. Follow path in wood before passing house on right at entry to Godden Green. Go straight across roadway onto wide track following footpath sign. Go down this track with stables to left. Emerge onto public road in Godden Green and turn right **with care** to return to the Buck's Head, along on right, thus completing Walk 16 **(A)**.

Track in Godden Wood approaching Point H

WALK 17

PENSHURST - WAT STOCK - HILL HOATH - CHIDDINGSTONE

You are advised to wear bright clothing on this walk as there is a short stretch of difficult road-walking beyond Point H	Start from - The LeicesterArms, Penshurst TN11 8BT Tel: 01892 871 617 Length of walk: 5½ miles Approximate time: 3 hours

(A) Set out from the Leicester Arms Hotel, Penshurst, by turning left out of its front door. Go on pavement on left-hand side of road just beyond T-junction. Now turn right to cross road **with great care** and walk to the immediate right of the Village Hall to head out of the village on the busy B2176. Pass the Fir Tree House Tearooms on left and pass parking area along left-hand side of road, also pass private road to *Latymers* on left and bus stop just beyond.

(B) At end of parking area, turn left to go down surfaced, tree-bordered roadway, following public bridleway sign. *We shall now be following the* **Eden Valley Walk** *as far as Hill Hoath.* Pass World War II concrete strongpoint, down to right. Over bridge crossing the River Eden and ignore stile on left just beyond. Almost immediately fork right, off better-surfaced roadway onto a very pleasant track which soon starts a very long ascent. Track soon overhung with bushes and then trees. Pass wood on left with lovely views over to right. Enter hamlet of Wat Stock, passing farmhouse on left and keeping on track between farm buildings. Now back onto surfaced road, as we leave Wat Stock, passing further house on left. Woods now on both sides of the road. Look carefully for waymark post on right-hand side of road and turn right here to go through small metal gate to right of large metal gate. Go diagonally left across field following a hopefully well-defined path and aiming for opposite corner.

(C) Go through small metal gate and almost immediately bear right to go along right-hand side of public road. After 50 paces cross road **with great care** and go over stile onto wide path in wood. At end of wood, go through wooden kissing-gate beside large wooden gate and keep in same direction along gently rising track partly bordered by trees. Ignore path to right and keep straight on up path. Buildings of Hill Hoath visible ahead and top of Chiddingstone church tower visible well over to right. Path now comes less distinct but soon bears left onto definite track. Go through small wooden gate to right of large metal gate and veer right to go on grassy path. Soon re-join track and pass well to right of farm buildings as we enter hamlet of Hill Hoath. Keep on track with houses on both sides.

View northwards from our path near Wat Stock

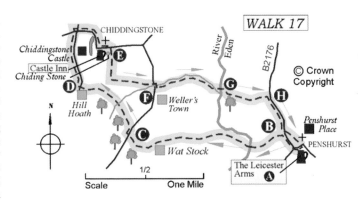

© Crown Copyright

(D) Veer right in Hill Hoath hamlet where there is a cart-shed ahead and pass further house on left. Go straight, not left, at small road junction just beyond this house. Now head out of Hill Hoath beside quiet public road soon passing its last house, which is on left. Pass by Chiddingstone Castle's orangery over to right and soon pass entrances to a few houses, both to right and left. Pass entrance to **Chiddingstone Castle** on right (*Only open at times - tel 01892 870 347 for details*). Turn right at X-rds where **Chiddingstone** entry is signed, onto busier road and walk along it **with great care**. Keep on road as it bends to right and go over bridge crossing the River Eden - dammed up here to form lake on right, this being part of Chiddingstone Castle's parkland. Turn left by the Castle Inn on right and the church up to left. Pass Post Office Shop on right and restaurant just beyond - a fine range of timbered buildings of great age. Pass school on right and then pass path on right leading to the Chiding Stone - an impressive outcrop of sandstone rock to which local legends are attached. (*If you wish to visit this do make sure to walk just beyond the first much smaller outcrop.*) Beyond turn to the Chiding Stone, watch carefully for a footpath signed on right, just beyond drive and very small green.

(E) Turn right onto this narrow, tree-shaded path. Pass one house over to right. Good views over to right as hedge on right becomes sporadic. Pass sports ground on left and then through gap (or small gate, if restored) into open country. Keep in same direction across field, soon starting to drop down towards valley. Towards bottom of slope veer left to follow left-hand edge of wood and then turn ninety degrees left to follow defined path across field - no sign.

The Chiding Stone - at Chiddingstone

Through gap in hedge to immediate left of large oak tree and over stile (if it has been rebuilt!). Veer slightly right to go across large field on well-defined path.

(F) At end of field go through large gap and turn right where Weller's Town is signed, to go along left-hand side of minor public road **with care**. After 50 paces, having crossed small stream, turn left off road, go over stile to right of large metal gate. Go along left-hand edge of field with trees and bushes to left. At end of this first field

45

The River Eden at Point G

go over stile to left of large metal gate and go along left-hand side of this second field. Over stile beside large metal gate and keep along left-hand side of this third, and very large field. Follow line of hedge on left as it bears to right and eventually go over stile to left of large metal gate. Keep along left-hand edge of this fourth field for only 40 paces before turning left to go over stile to left of large metal gate. Veer right across this fifth field following waymark's direction and soon aiming for waymark post on "bridge" over modest drainage ditch. Veer right by this waymark post to aim for small metal gate in bushes.

(G) Through this small gate and go over River Eden on footbridge. Immediately beyond bridge turn right to go along short, right-hand edge of field. Soon bear right onto ill-defined, grassy path leading towards wood, with River Eden just visible over to right. Watch for this with great care - it could easily be missed. After about 65 paces, turn left onto definite path into wood. Now starting a long climb which continues after we leave wood. Beyond wood keep up left-hand edge of field with hedge to immediate left. Fine views over to right, across the Eden Valley to the wooded country we passed through on our outward journey. At top of slope pass barn on right with track to right just beyond it. But keep in same direction, now going along right-hand side of next field. Pass wood on right, ignoring small wooden gate into it. Pass old garden wall on right and, at end of field, bear slightly right onto short, narrow path through woodlands before going carefully down steps with handrail.

(H) At bottom of steps, turn right to go along right-hand side of busy B2176 **with very great care, keeping to right-hand side of road. Come to a halt each time a vehicle approaches and keep well into the side. If in company, go in single-file.** Pass lodge on right. Pass entries to Culver Lodge and The Old Orchard on right. Now use the very narrow grass verge on right. Penshurst entry signed. Pass entrance gates to Penshurst Place over to left (not for public use) and after a few paces **cross road with very great care when you have view of oncoming traffic both to fore and aft**. Keep in same direction along narrow grass verge on left-hand side of road before turning left through metal kissing-gate into Penshurst's parkland. Veer away from line of road heading towards right-hand end of hedge fronting Penshurst Place and towards church tower just beyond. Go through kissing-gate into churchyard and go through this passing the church's south porch. Keep down path to leave churchyard beneath cottage and down short courtyard. *Unless you wish to visit Penshurst Place by turning left and going through gateway beyond,* **turn right** to go along pavement above busy road in Penshurst. Pass attractive timbered house on right and, **when safe,** cross road to arrive at the Leicester Arms Hotel thus completing Walk 17 **(A)**.

WALK 18

EDENBRIDGE - LYDENS FARM - MARSH GREEN - EDENBRIDGE

(A) Set out from the Eden Valley Museum, Edenbridge, turning right to go southwards, down the High Street. Pass the Old Crown Inn, on right, cross the road and almost immediately turn left to go up Church Street. *We shall now follow the course of the **Eden Valley Walk** until reaching Point **C**.* Pass church lych-gate and church keeping along left-hand side of road before turning left through iron gates into cemetery. Keep straight through cemetery and then turn right and left to go through kissing-gate, following sign - *Eden Valley Walk.* Keep on path which soon turns left and then turn right on to Churchfield Road. Soon turn right to go beside wider road and almost immediately turn left to go up sloping, surfaced track, curving to right to cross railway line.

Start from - The Eden Valley Museum,
72, High Street, Edenbridge TN8 5NR
Tel: 01732 868 102
Length of walk: 6 miles
Approximate time: 3½ hours

(B) Beyond railway bridge keep straight down track overhung by trees and at its end keep in same direction to go through kissing-gate. Keep in same direction through bushy area passing pond on left and then go down left-hand side of large field. At far left-hand end of field go over stile beneath large oak tree. Keep in same direction to go down left-hand edge of next field with hedge to immediate left, following waymark's direction. Over small footbridge beside wider bridge crossing wide ditch and keep in same direction across centre of next field. Soon keep to immediate right of fence on left. Over another wooden footbridge at end of field and through kissing-gate. Bear slightly right to go up hill across field following waymark's direction. Keep just to right of clump of trees sheltering a pond. Keep in same direction, now heading for gap with gate in hedgeline ahead. Over stile to right of large metal gate and fork right to go diagonally down across field following the right-hand of two waymarks here. At end of projecting hedgeline on right, turn right to go down track along right-hand edge of field. Where track bends to right, veer slightly left to go through kissing-gate to left of large metal gate. Keep on track as it now enters wooded area.

(C) Over bridge crossing the little River Eden and follow track as it passes large yew hedge to right. Pass small wooden gate on right. Turn left on track by pond on right and half-timbered building ahead. This area is part of Delaware Farm. Pass modern barn on left and pass houses on both sides of drive. Turn right **with care** on to public road.

Church Street, Edenbridge

47

Pass house on right and after 50 paces turn left to go over small wooden bridge in hedge-gap and go straight across field aiming for steps up railway embankment. On reaching bottom of steps, do not go up them, but turn left to go along wooded right-hand edge of field with embankment now immediately to right. Search carefully for gap on right leading to tall underbridge beneath the embankment. Well before reaching cross-hedge ahead, turn right through this gap and go through underbridge beneath embankment. Veer slightly left beyond underbridge to go almost due south across centre of field aiming for gap in trees ahead. At end of field, go through

gateway and veer right onto public road. Go along this road with **care**, soon ignoring track to Oast Farm on left.

(D) Pass Lydens Farm farmyard on left with its attractive oast. *We leave the course of the **Eden Valley Walk** here, which goes to the left through the farmyard.* Keep on along minor road and soon pass entrance on left to Lydens Farmhouse. Pass Lydens Cottage on left and after 30 paces ignore footpath fingerpost on left. Keep on this minor road until meeting the B2026. **Cross this very busy road with great care** and go over stile to right of large wooden gate. Go down short track with hedge and trees to immediate right and buildings over to left. At end of track go over stile to right of large wooden gate and turn right to go along right-hand edge of field with hedge to right. Towards the end of field ignore indentation of hedge to right and aim for gap in tree-line ahead. Through large metal gate in gap and keep in same direction along right-hand edge of field. At end of field go over stile in far right-hand corner and over surfaced roadway to go through kissing gate. Veer very slightly left to go across lower end of next field. *The roadway that we have just crossed follows the course of the **Roman Road** that ran from the Watling Street in Peckham to the South Downs just to the east of Lewes.* Go through metal kissing-gate to right of large wooden gate and through belt of trees just beyond. Keep along right-hand edge of field with hedge and trees to immediate right. Over stile in cross-hedge and keep along lower edge of field with woods to right, but towards its end veer up to left ignoring small wooden gate on right and keep up field with its wooded edge still to right. Go beneath large oak tree and over stile well to the right of large wooden gate.

(E) Now turn sharp right on to surfaced road (sign - *Bridleway*). *The next section of road runs along a causeway, which acts as a dam forming a large pool just visible to left. This once provided a head of water for Christmas Mill.* Pass Christmas Mill Cottage on right and Christmas Place on left. Where road turns to right go straight across and go over stile beside large metal gate. Keep along right-hand edge of field with hedge to immediate right. Well before the end of field turn right through wide gap in hedge (watch out for this with care) and go along top, left-hand edge of next field with hedge and trees

48

to immediate left. Go over stile in top, left-hand corner of field and go straight across centre of next field on hopefully well-defined path. Splendid views ahead, over the Wealden country to the distant Greensand ridge. Soon start to drop downwards and at bottom end of field go onto track before turning left at crossing of tracks. Go along this partly-surfaced track entering **Marsh Green**.

(F) At end of track, with the Wheatsheaf Inn facing us (*Tel: 01732 864 091*), turn right **with very great care to go alongside the very busy B2028**. Keep along pathway through Marsh Green, but well before it veers to right by village green cross road **with very great care** and go along minor road to left of green and to right of church. Pass useful bench on right beneath oak tree. Pass play area on right and where road bends to right turn left to go through kissing-gate and follow fngerpost's direction across centre of large field, aiming for kissing-gate just to left of large metal gate. Cross surfaced track beyond kissing-gate and through second kissing-gate. Veer right following waymark's direction across corner of field. Go through kissing-gate to right of large metal gate and follow waymark's direction down right-hand edge of next field. Through kissing-gate below oak tree in right-hand corner of field and emerge through bushes into very small field. Almost immediately go through second kissing-gate to left of large metal gate and bear right following waymark's direction across right-hand corner of next field. Keep in same direction across next field and go to left of stile beneath large oak tree. Veer further left ignoring two large metal gates to locate wooden kissing-gate just to their left - and not easy to spot. Go through kissing-gate and keep along path between wood on left and fenced field on right. Keep along path eventually passing metal gates both to left and right. After about 90 paces go through wooden kissing-gate and on to path within narrow belt of trees. Keep on path as it bends to left by large pond on right. Immediately beyond pond ignore path coming in from left and keep bearing right. Pass buildings on right (part of Edenbridge Memorial Hospital, but not apparent).

(G) Soon turn left to go beside the very busy B2026 **with very great care** at this, our entry to **Edenbridge**. Keep on left-hand footpath beside the B2026 which follows the course of the **Roman Road** that we crossed earlier. Soon cross **with very great care** to the right-hand side of the road. Keep on pavement passing to the right of large roundabout and over bridge crossing the River Eden. Now cross to left-hand side of Edenbridge High Street. Pass timbered buildings to left, and the King and Queen Inn on right. Pass small road up to church on right, pass the Old Crown Inn on left, with its signboard over the centre of the street, and arrive at the Eden Valley Museum on left, thus completing Walk 18 **(A)**.

Our path heading for Marsh Green

WALK 19

SEVENOAKS WEALD - BORE PLACE - WICKHURST

(A) Set out from the Windmill Inn, **Sevenoaks Weald**, by turning left out of its front door and going up Long Barn Road. Walk along pavement on right of road or along edge of wide village green parallel to road. Pass attractive village sign on edge of green, opposite to school. At end of green keep steeply down beside Long Barn Road with houses to left and woods to

Start from - The Windmill Inn, Sevenoaks Weald TN14 6PN
Tel: 01732 463 330
Length of walk: 6 miles
Approximate time: 3 hours

right. Just beyond last house on left, which is *Long Barn*, and where road bends to right, turn left onto path with wooden fencing to left and bushes to right, following public footpath fingerpost. Almost immediately go through squeeze-stile ahead, ignoring path to left. Go straight across field on path sheltered by two oak trees. Good view backwards to *Long Barn*. On meeting woods ahead veer right to go along left-hand edge of field with wood now on left. Over small footbridge into next field, and soon bear left into wood before bearing right onto woodland path. Keep on this path along narrow belt of woodlands and at its end ---

(B) --- go over public road **with care** and go over stile and footbridge following public footpath fingerpost. Go along right-hand edge of field with fenced driveway to immediate right. Well before end of field go over stile beside metal gate and plank footbridge just beyond. Veer slightly right to go across remainder of field. Near end of field drop downwards to go over stile into narrow belt of woodland and over footbridge crossing small stream. Immediately over another stile and go straight up, across field to locate small, difficult to spot footbridge in another narrow belt of woodlands ahead. Keep across next field in same direction and go over stile in cross-fence. Now cross track and go over second stile. Keep in same direction across next field and go through squeeze-stile before crossing track and going over stile and footbridge. Now turn right to follow right-hand edge of field with woods to immediate right. Ignore footpath into woods on right, after going through squeeze-stile.

(C) Keep on path along edge of wood as it bends to right (*this is Eight Acre Wood, but not indicated here*). But before reaching next corner, turn left to take short-cut across field on hopefully well-defined path. Follow path as it soon re-joins woodlands on right and soon turn right to go over stile and footbridge in corner of wood. Bear right to go

Springtime on the green at Sevenoaks Weald

along right-hand edge of field with wood to immediate right. At corner of field go onto path between wooden fencing on left and woods on right. At end of wood on right emerge into field and bear left to go diagonally across field aiming for low-voltage power-pole. Buildings of Hale Oak Farm just visible well over to left. On reaching power-pole go through gap in fence and bear right to go along grassy track with fence on both sides. Go through possibly gated gap and over slight stream. At end of field do not go through gap, but turn left to go along right-hand edge of field and after only 40 paces turn right to go through small metal gate and over wooden footbridge. Climb steps and

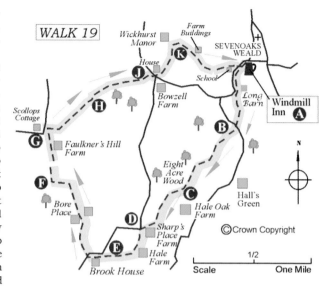

go diagonally up, across field aiming just to right of farm buildings which soon come into view. Keep on track to right of farm buildings and almost immediately bear right keeping on track. On reaching further farm buildings ahead bear right, down track and go beside large metal gate.

(D) After 40 paces turn left **with care** onto minor public road and where road bends to right with houses of Sharp's Place up to left, go straight up slope following public footpath fingerpost. Go over stile beside large metal gate and along grassy path with hedge to left. Soon go over stile beside large metal gate and keep straight down across field with fence to immediate left. In corner of field go through kissing-gate and keep along edge of next field. Ignore stile on left, with buildings of Hale Farm visible down to left. At this point go diagonally right, across field aiming for far right-hand corner (no waymark). Go into bushes and through gap into next field. Turn left to follow left-hand edge for a short distance and turn right in corner, ignoring small wooden gate ahead. Go down left-hand edge of field and, half-way down field, at end of wood on left, turn left to go over easily-missed stile. Go diagonally across field on hopefully well-defined path, just to left of line of power-cables above. Go over stile into narrow belt of woodland down short but very slippery bank. Go over small footbridge and onto minor   public road.

(E) Turn left to go along road **with care** passing house over to right and then one on left. Pass entry to Brook House on left and where road bends to left, turn right to follow sign - *Bore Place only and Bridleway.* Go along surfaced driveway heading for Bore Place. Through two small wooden gates beside two cattle-grids keeping on driveway. Now pass farm buildings over to left and enter **Bore Place**. Pass more buildings on both sides and eventually bear left to go through gap by low wall below weatherboarded house. Now go up brick steps and through small metal gate. Head up roadway just to right of small building with tile-hung gable-end, leaving **Bore Place**. Continue up surfaced roadway but after passing white-painted house over to right, go onto rougher surfaced track. Soon, where there is a gate ahead, turn left to follow track upwards. Now pass wood on left just beyond top of slope.

A distant view of the Greensand ridge from Point F

(F) Turn right, ignoring gate and stile ahead and keep along track. Fine views from here. Track soon becomes tree-shaded and then enters woodlands. Pass buildings of Faulkner's Hill Farm over to right. Track now starts to drop downwards. Ignore driveway to right and go down to minor road with house immediately ahead.

(G) Turn right **with care** onto this minor public road, passing house on right and several houses on left. Turn right, off road, opposite *1, Scollops Cottage* on left, following public footpath fingerpost and go over stile. Go up along right-hand edge of field avoiding probably obstructed hollow-way under trees on right. Pass house over to right and follow fence-line on right as it descends to stile below tree. Go over this stile and over a second one immediately beyond. Go along left-hand side of field with woods on left. At end of field go over stile well to right of large metal gate. Keep in same direction to go diagonally across field aiming to left of three oak trees. Fine views over to left of rolling country stretching away to the wooded slopes of the Greensand ridge. Over stile to left of oak trees and keep in same direction to go diagonally across large field aiming for far right-hand corner.

(H) Go through wide gap in far corner of field and turn right to go three-quarters around pond below trees. Now go through large metal gate in cross-hedge and turn left to go down left-hand edge of field with hedge and trees to immediate left. At bottom left-hand corner of field go through gap in bushes and over waymarked stile. Keep along right-hand edge of field with hedge and trees to immediate right. At end of field ignore large and small gates to right and go onto track through gap in cross-hedge. Keep along right-hand edge of this, next field with woodland to right. Near end of woodland on right, watch carefully for small, and easily missed gap in hedge on right leading to small footbridge. Go over this bridge and head diagonally right up across field eventually going just to right of woods projecting from left. Go through gap in woods on left with bushes and trees to right and go diagonally across large field. (*If necessary turn right to follow to immediate left of lower edge of field before turning left to cross*

52

rest of field.) When reaching the top of field near its right-hand end search carefully for small gap in bushes and trees. Go through this gap into very narrow belt of woodland and keep in same direction to go down across narrow field.

(J) Through kissing-gate and turn right onto minor public road. Go along this **with care**, and just beyond white-painted house on left,

Sevenoaks Weald Church - to the north of the Windmill Inn

turn left to go through small metal gate following public footpath fingerpost. Go straight down field aiming just to left of hedge projecting from right. Go along bottom of field with hedge now on immediate right. Go through small metal gate in right-hand corner of field and keep along right-hand edge of next field with fence to immediate right. Through small metal gate below oak tree and, almost immediately,

View from the west doorway,
Sevenoaks Weald Church

go through a second small metal gate. Keep along right-hand edge of next field with hedge and trees to immediate right. Near end of field bear round to right to go through squeeze-stile in cross-fence. Bear diagonally left following waymark direction, and, at top of field, go through large wooden gate. Turn right to go along concrete roadway with Wickhurst Manor visible up to left. (*We have now joined the* **Greensand Way**, *but this will have no significance for us on this walk.*)

(K) At end of concrete roadway, turn right to go along surfaced road with entrance to Cedar House on right. (*We shall now follow this roadway into Sevenoaks Weald, but a few details of the route are also included.*) Pass low farm buildings on left and onto less well-surfaced track. Ignore footpath to right. Pass one or two houses on right and finally pass school buildings on right. At end of buildings, bear right and then turn left to go along pavement beside road, Soon arrive at the Windmill Inn, on opposite side of road beyond village green, thus completing Walk 19 **(A)**.

WALK 20

PENSHURST - LEIGH - HAYSDEN COUNTRY PARK - TONBRIDGE

(A) Set out from the Leicester Arms Hotel, Penshurst, by turning right out of its front door. Go on pavement on right-hand side of road until it is safe to cross **(with great care)** to pavement on left-hand side. Go along pavement passing half-timbered house and then turn left to go up small courtyard and

> Start from - The Leicester Arms,
> Penshurst TN11 8BT
> Tel: 01892 871 617
> Length of walk: 10 miles
> Approximate time: 5½ hours

beneath tile-hung cottage into churchyard. Go along left-hand edge of churchyard passing south porch and west door below the tower. Keep along left-hand edge and leave churchyard through kissing-gate. Go across parkland to left of Penshurst Place but soon veer right at Y-junction of paths indicated by waymarks on post. Go through two kissing-gates to cross private entry drive and keep down initially surfaced path at the start of a long, wide avenue. But soon veer right, away from the avenue following lightly-defined grassy path, aiming to left of large trees and then to a kissing-gate just to the right of a short bushy hedge. Go through kissing-gate and turn right following footpath fingerpost. Now keep to immediate left of fence, passing a series of clipped yews and a lake just visible beyond it. Keep following to left of fence and then go through small metal gate beside large metal gate. *Note base of large tree up to left, this is the Sidney Oak, which is believed to be nearly 500 years old, and is said to have been planted on the birth of the poet Sir Philip Sidney in the 16th century. It was named one of the Top 50 Great British Trees, by The Tree Council (UK), in 2002 to honour the Queen's Golden Jubilee.* Veer left to go gently up hillside on a very lightly-defined, grassy path with individual trees soon closing in from both sides. Go through small metal gate beside large metal gate and go quite steeply, straight up beautiful, broad avenue.

(B) At crossing of tracks at top of rise turn right to go along another equally lovely, broad avenue, following footpath fingerpost. Cross surfaced track and almost immediately go through gap in cross-fence before continuing along avenue. Ignore footpath signed to left and soon go through large metal gate at end of avenue. Keep in almost the same direction to go along track across field soon veering away from its right-hand to its left-hand edge. In left-hand corner of field go down track into

Avenue in Penshurst Park, just beyond Point B

woodland with fence to immediate left. Through gateway with possible metal gate and keep down rutted track, which could be muddy in winter.

(C) At end of track turn left onto busy minor road and walk down it **with very great care**. Soon entering outskirts of Leigh and pass Leigh entry sign. Go under right-hand side of underbridge beneath

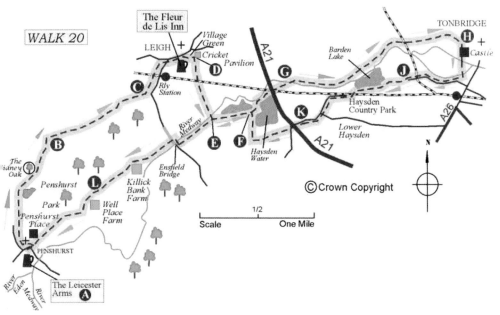

WALK 20

railway embankment. Entries to railway station on right. Now, thankfully, onto pavement just beyond. Turn right onto the even busier B2027 by the Fleur de Lis Inn on right. Pass Village Hall and Post Office Shop on right. Pass path to church, up steep bank to left but turn right, down road which skirts large cricket field on village green, now on our left. There are helpful benches under trees to left. Bear round to left, ignoring turns to right, and follow edge of green until arriving at cricket pavilion on right-hand side of road.

(D) Now turn right immediately before cricket pavilion, into Green View Avenue. Go to the end of Green View Avenue and go through kissing-gate onto track which is also a public footpath. Go down track and through underbridge beneath high railway embankment. Go through metal kissing-gate beside large metal gate and keep in same direction along right-hand edge of small field with fence to immediate right. Through gap in sporadic cross-hedge crossing small ditch and keep in same direction across centre of large field following lightly--defined grassy pathway and soon aiming for near end of footbridge framed by bushes. Over this substantial footbridge crossing the River Medway. Bear left beyond bridge to follow narrow path into woodland. Almost immediately bearing right by small stream and ---

A quiet place to relax beside Haysden Water

55

(E1) --- and at tree-sheltered intersection of paths, turn left onto the **Eden Valley Walk** and National Cycle Network No 12. (*But turn right to follow the Eden Valley Walk if you wish to use the return route - see Point* **E2**, *below.*) Now keep along tree-shaded embankment with boggy woodlands below, on either side. Be aware of cyclists with whom we share much of this remaining route.

Tonbridge Castle

(F1) Keep straight, not right, at junction of paths, temporarily leaving Cycle Route 12, but keeping on the Eden Valley Walk. (*We shall arrive at this point on our return route - see* **F2** *below.*) Almost immediately turn left to go over footbridge and keep straight ahead on main path beyond, ignoring slight path to right. Now starting to pass around the shore of the large lake, Haysden Water, over to our right. Pass well to right of railway embankment before going below the embankment of the very busy A21. Keep on path between Haysden Water on right and road viaduct on left and near end of viaduct go up concrete road. Near top of rise turn left to go along top of flood barrier beneath end of viaduct.

(G) Beyond viaduct bear right down flood barrier embankment and follow sign *Bridle Route*, by going along grassy path with trees and bushes on both sides - this is known as The Straight Mile. At top of slight rise turn sharp left to go over small footbridge before veering left to keep on main path. Eventually turn right to go over second footbridge and keep on path following *Eden Valley Walk* waymark. Bear right beyond squeeze-stile and turn right following sign *Barden Lake and Car Park*. Immediately bear left to go under railway embankment on a very narrow path. Bear right at intersection of paths following sign - *Barden Lake*. Soon turn left to cross large footbridge over the River Medway and turn right to follow path along left-hand edge of field, with the Medway running parallel to our right. Follow path as it goes into bushes or along field edges, but always parallel with the Medway. Path eventually runs just to the left of the Medway. Go straight ahead at crossing of paths with Lucifer Bridge just to right. Go straight over footbridge crossing stream and almost immediately over second footbridge and turn right (sign - *Cycle Route 12*). Over footbridge and bear slightly right (sign - *Cycle Route 12*). Soon go over footbridge beneath low railway embankment and keep straight, not left, temporarily leaving cycleway. Keep along path with large sportsfields to right and hedge to left. Soon rejoin cycleway and sportsfields now on both sides. Ignore path to right and keep on cycleway, Footpath and cycleway are parallel with each other - choose footpath when possible to avoid cyclists! Follow path as it curves round to right following edge of sportsfield. Pass large, modern building on left and bear left onto surfaced road with large car park over to right. Pass school on left and veer round to right. Go to right just beyond bend and go up path across grass with car park to left. Bear left at end and soon bear right to go into the impressive gatehouse of Tonbridge Castle.

(H) Go through Tonbridge Castle gatehouse and bear right to go down path below the castle mound and at bottom of slope turn sharp right to follow sign - *Eden Valley Walk.* Follow path below the mound and then turn left to go over footbridge crossing the River Medway (sign - *Eden Valley Walk*). Pass swimming pool building on left and at its end veer left to go over footbridge. Beyond bridge keep straight ahead at crossing of paths to go along left-hand edge of large sportsfield, with tennis courts on left and children's play area on right. Veer left beyond children's play area and go over footbridge before turning right to go along path to left of river. Veer left near end of path and turn right to go along right-hand side of Barden Road, going past Barden Stores. Just beyond bend turn right into Barden Park Road. Follow road as it bends to right to go over railway bridge and keep right into Audley Avenue. Over small X-rds and then ignore turning on right to Alders Avenue.

(J) At entry to Audley Rise leave road and go straight ahead to enter small car park for Haysden Country Park. Turn left just beyond car park passing Haysden Country Park notice board on left. Follow surfaced path as it gently veers to right and fork right (sign - *Haysden Country Park*). Soon join wider path and over footbridge before bearing left to follow the left-hand shore of the large Barden Lake. Fork right, leaving cycleway to go on footpath, still above the shore of Barden Lake with several welcome benches. Go beneath large willow tree and beyond this the lake shore takes a sharp turn to the right. Soon turn left to go along tree-shaded track (sign - *Toilets and Play Area*). Go under bridge beneath railway and bear left onto path beside public road leaving Haysden Country Park. Turn right **with great care** at T-junction with public road. Go straight, not left by Acorn House (*used to be the Royal Oak Inn*) and bear right and then left to keep on public road. Noise from the A21's busy traffic now becoming apparent.

(K) Go under bridge beneath the A21 and after 70 paces turn right at road junction. After 15 paces turn left onto bridleway which

Barden Lake, beyond Point J

is on Cycle Route 12 (sign - *Penshurst - 3½*). Ignore footpath signed to right but almost immediately turn right to go through squeeze-stile and follow path along right-hand side of field with fence to left and hedge to right (*still on Cycle Route 12*). Through squeeze-stile into wood and ---

(F2) --- turn left at junction of paths thus joining our outward route and the Eden Valley Walk (*see* **F1** *above*) (sign - *Penshurst*). Keep along tree-shaded embankment in woods. Go straight over crossing of paths at **E2** (sign - *Cycle Route 12*) and keep along tree-shaded path. On meeting fence across track, veer left up slope and bear right, still in woodland, but now just within its left-hand edge. Soon go up another slope and leave woodland following path with fence to left and woodland to right. Turn right onto public road and go along it **with great care**. Soon go over Ensfield Bridge crossing the River Medway. Soon turn left off public road (Fingerpost Sign - *Penshurst*) and follow track, initially going

The River Medway from Ensfield Bridge

parallel with public road. Soon bear left to follow long and rather boring concrete road. (*Beware of the silent approach of cyclists - we are still on National Cycle Route 12*). Pass attractive poplar plantation and start long steady climb up concrete roadway. Pass entry to Killick Bank Farm on left. Fine open views behind us and also to our left.

(L) Our road eventually flattens out and where it bends to the left, go straight ahead onto track, leaving the Cycle Route, but still on the **Eden Valley Walk**. Keep on track along left-hand edge of field and in its corner go through squeeze-stile to left of metal gate. Veer left following Eden Valley Walk's waymark arrow on well-defined path across field, soon going steeply down bank. At bottom of field go through squeeze-stile and along left-hand edge of next field. Before end of field turn left to go through squeeze-stile before turning right to go along estate roadway re-joining Cycle Route 12. Keep along this roadway, passing pool on right and car park for Penshurst Place well beyond. Pass long estate wall on right and, keeping on roadway, go through archway beyond. Keep on pavement to right of busy public road at this, our entry to Penshurst village. Pass courtyard entry to church on right and attractive timbered house just beyond on right. **When safe,** cross road to arrive at the Leicester Arms Hotel thus completing Walk 20 **(A)**.

Courtyard at the entry to Penshurst Churchyard

BIDBOROUGH E-4 Village on a high sandstone ridge to the south-west of **Tonbridge.** Bidborough has a a small church, much of which dates back to the 13th century. This has a stubby shingled spire and although its interior was much altered in the 19th century it retains a surprisingly pleasing atmosphere. There is an impressive tower arch beyond which a great clock pendulum swings back and forth in front of the west window - a most unusual feature. Do not miss the handsome monument in the churchyard to the Countess of Darnley by the well-known early-19th-century sculptor, Richard Westmacott. There are fine views in almost every direction from Bidborough's lofty, windswept churchyard.

BORE PLACE D-2 Here is an organic dairy farm with a conference and study centre organised by The Commonwork Educational Trust. Its educational programmes *"combine social enterprise with work towards a more just and sustainable world"*. Bore Place is on the course of our **Walk 19** and in addition, the Bore Place Field Trail is described in a useful leaflet usually obtainable from its Reception Office. For more information see www.commonwork.org

Bough Beech Reservoir from the road to its east

BOUGH BEECH C-3 A hamlet just to the south of the large **Bough Beech Reservoir** with an attractive inn, the Wheatsheaf (*Tel: 01732 700 100*) but little else of any great interest.

BOUGH BEECH RESERVOIR AND VISITOR CENTRE C-2 An attractive stretch of water with bird-watching possibilities from the road leading across part of its north-

eastern edge. Birds likely to be spotted here include Mandarin Duck, Great Crested Grebe and Grey Heron. Near its north-western end, there is an interesting Visitor Centre run by the Kent Wildlife Trust. This is housed in an oast and has interesting displays and a gift shop. Coffee and light refreshments available. It has a car park, and is also on the course of our **Walk 10**.

The Visitor Centre, Bough Beech Reservoir

CHARCOTT D-3 Quiet hamlet in attractive rolling country north of **Chiddingstone Causeway**, with a pleasant inn - the Greyhound (*Tel: 01892 870 275*). Charcott is on the course of our **Walk 14**.

CHARTWELL (NT) B-2 From their purchase in 1922 this was, for more than forty years, the much-loved home of Sir Winston and Lady Churchill. The tall red-brick, mid-Victorian house was greatly improved and extended by the Churchills. It stands on the southern slopes of the Greensand ridge, above a valley with two lakes and there are distant views of the Weald beyond. Inside the house the main living rooms are kept as though the great man had only recently left, with note pads beside the bed and papers on the desk. In other rooms his uniforms and decorations are on display together with many gifts and mementoes. Some of Sir Winston's paintings hang on the walls and many more can be seen in his studio in the grounds. It is possible to walk in Lady Churchill's Rose Garden and beside the lakes that her husband created. There is also at least one woodland walk. *Restaurant. Shop. Entrance by timed ticket only (no booking available). www.nationaltrust.org.uk/chartwell for many more details.* Chartwell lies near the course of our **Walk 1** and is also not far from the course of our **Walk 12**.

Chartwell - the home of Sir Winston Churchill

Chiddingstone Church

CHIDDINGSTONE C-3 The row of typically Kentish brick and half-timbered buildings opposite the church includes the ancient and full-of-character Castle Inn (*Tel: 01892 870 247*), which has been in the care of the National Trust since 1939. Originally the main road continued straight past the inn to a manor house known as High Street House, but at the very end of the 18th century Henry Streatfeild, head of a the family of prosperous Wealden ironmasters which had owned the manor since the early 1500's, created the present 'castle'. He did this by refacing the existing building with sandstone and adding Gothick towers, turrets and battlements (*see below*). At the same time he diverted the road, made a lake and landscaped the park. Chiddingstone Church, with its impressive tower, is largely 14th-century in origin, but it was much restored in the early 17th century following a major fire. There are several Streatfeild monuments within but none is exceptional. There is however an impressive 18th-century Streatfeild family mausoleum in the churchyard. The Chiding Stone, an impressive outcrop of sandstone, is reached by a path leaving the road off to the right beyond the school. *Follow this path as it runs behind the school and* **go just beyond** *the first much smaller outcrop before reaching the Chiding Stone itself.* Despite tales relating to villagers being taken here to be `chided' it is probable that the place-name Chiddingstone is derived from a local Saxon chief named Cedd and that this was his *'ing'* or settlement. Chiddingstone is on the course of our **Walk 17.**

CHIDDINGSTONE CASTLE C-3 Standing in pleasant parkland with a lake in the valley below, this neo-Gothick castle was built by Henry Streatfeild at the very end of the 18th century (see above). The castle has been in the hands of a charitable trust for many years and houses the fascinating and very varied collection of art and artefacts assembled by its last private owner, the late Denys Eyre. These collections include Japanese lacquer and Samurai armour, Buddhist objects and Egyptian treasures. lso Stuart and Jacobite paintings. *Tearoom and Gift Shop. Tel: 01892 870 347*

CHIDDINGSTONE CAUSEWAY D-3 Strung out along the B2027, this village grew in size in the latter half of the 19th century due partly to its proximity to the confusingly named *Penshurst* Railway Station. It has an inn, the Little Brown Jug (*Tel: 01892 870 318*) and a late-Victorian church designed by John Bentley, better known as the architect of Westminster Cathedral.

Chiddingstone Castle

This church has a pleasingly simple interior with a broad sanctuary below an east window with complex stone tracery and beautifully-coloured stained glass. There appears to be no sign of a probable medieval causeway crossing low ground here, although this must have been the original reason for this village's name.

Cricket was the other rather unusual cause of this village's growth. Between 1760 and 1994 bats and balls were made, first in Penshurst and then, in 1841, Timothy Duke moved his firm to Chiddingstone Causeway. Duke's cricket balls are still produced today but they are no longer made here in the Eden Valley.

There was once a small airfield, to the north of the village, and to the south of neighbouring **Charcott** hamlet. This was first used by the RFC in the First World War and by he RAF during the Second. Known as Penshurst Airfield, it was closed in 1936 when the ground lease expired, but it was re-opened during the Second World War as an Emergency Landing Ground and as a base for light aircraft including Austers. It finally closed in May 1946.

CHIDDINGSTONE HOATH C-4 Hamlet with an attractive little inn at Hoath Corner, just to its north, the Rock (*Tel: 01892 870 296*). The nearby Italianate mansion of Stonewall Park is surrounded by beautiful parkland and is privately owned. It does however usually open its lovely gardens twice a year as part of the National Gardens Scheme.

COWDEN B-4 A close-knit village near the Sussex border with a number of white weatherboarded and half-timbered houses. The tile-hung Fountain Inn (*Tel: 01342 850 528*) is well worth a visit. The medieval church was, like so many of Kent's churches, much restored in the 19th century, but its cool, white-washed interior is very pleasant. It also sustained some damage during the Second World War and one of

One of many attractive houses at Cowden

the stained glass windows in the nave was inserted as a thanksgiving for the church's survival in the war. The attractively- shingled steeple dates back to the 14th century and rests on six massive posts which are visible within the nave. There is a fine Jacobean pulpit with tester and there are several iron tomb slabs in the churchyard reminding us that Cowden was very much in the heart of the Wealden iron-founding country. Our **Walk 13** starts from the Fountain Inn (se above).

South doorway, Cowden Church

There were at least two important iron foundries in the Cowden area in the 17th century and both shot and shell were being supplied to the government in the 1690s. Cannon were being manufactured here in the first part of the 18th century, but it is thought that production finally ceased in about 1770, no doubt due to competition from the new iron manufacturers in the North Country. Cowden's foundries were situated in the valley to its west and Furnace Pond remains as evidence of the water-power once required to drive the great forge hammers. Passing between the village and Furnace Pond, in the vicinity of Kitford Bridge, is the course of the **Roman Road,** now known as the London to Lewes Way. **Walk 13** starts from Cowden's Fountain Inn and **Walk 15** also passes through the village.

CROCKHAM HILL B-2 There are far-reaching views over the Weald from this small village below the wooded slopes of the Greensand ridge. The Royal Oak Inn (*Tel: 01732 866 335*), which serves locally-brewed ales, is on the main B269 road but the church lies a little to its east. This early-Victorian building is noted for its monument to Octavia Hill - whose effigy in white marble reclines on a large tomb chest. Octavia was one of the four founders of the National Trust in 1895 and she was also a formidable social housing reformer. Born at Wisbech in 1838, she spent her final years at Larkfield, a house in Crockham Hill and although she was offered a final resting place in Westminster Abbey she opted for the church in her village. She died in 1912, but after more than a hundred years, we remain very much in her debt. Do not miss the Octavia Hill Memorial Window to the right of the entrance door. Octavia Hill and the National Trust's Oak Leaf symbol are both depicted. Our **Walk 1** starts from Crockham Hill and in its early stage passes the church.

Memorial Window to Octavia Hill, Crockham Hill Church

DRY HILL LOCAL NATURE RESERVE D-1 This is off Dry Hill Lane, to the south of the A25 west of Sevenoaks and the turn-off is just to the west of the large interchange with the M25 approach road. There was once a large quarry here, but this has now reverted to woodland, and there is an extensive grassy area suitable for picnicking close to its car park. The nearby rocky outcrops are all linked by a number of paths.

EDENBRIDGE B-3 This small market town has been considerably enlarged by much London overspill housing on its northern edge. But despite this it has retained much of its character, with friendly shops and inns and a thriving market on each Thursday morning. Its long High Street follows the exact course of the **Roman Road** now known as the London to Lewes Way. There are a number of attractive old houses and shops, most of which are near the lower end of the High Street, not far from the bridge over the little River Eden. The High Street is spanned by the Crown Inn's overhanging signboard and Edenbridge's very interesting Eden Valley Museum (*Tel: 01732 868 102*) is close by. The church is quietly tucked away just to the east of the High Street. It has its origins in the 13th and 14th centuries, but like most churches in this area, was

Church Street, Edenbridge

63

heavily restored by the Victorians. To explore Edenbridge in more detail obtain the leaflet *Edenbridge Historic Town Trail* from the Eden Valley Museum or from the Information Centre behind it. Further leaflets describing walks near Edenbridge are also obtainable here. Our **Walks 7 and 18** both start from the Eden Valley Museum.

EDEN, RIVER C-3 etc.
Rising near the village of Titsey in Surrey, the little Eden first flows south-wards before turning east to enter Kent near Haxted Mill. It then flows through Edenbridge, and derives its name from this town which used to be called "E a d e l m e s b r e g g e" (*Eadhelm's Bridge*) in Old English. It then flows eastwards through wooded Wealden country to join the Medway near **Penshurst**. The owners of Hever and Chiddingstone

The River Eden at Edenbridge

Castles both harnessed its waters to create lakes in their parks. See also the **Eden Valley Walk**, below.

EDEN VALLEY WALK B-3, etc. - its course being marked on our Key Map. Although, officially this long-distance path starts in meadows near Cernes Farm (GR 426 445), south of Haxted Mill, thereby linking with the Vanguard Way, although most people will prefer to start from **Edenbridge**. From here the path heads generally eastwards keeping as close as possible to the course of the River Eden as far as its confluence with the River Medway near **Penshurst**. It then follows close to the course of the Medway to end at **Tonbridge** Castle, having covered a total distance of about 15 miles. Our **Walks 11, 18 and 20** follow sections of the Eden Valley Walk. It is also described in leaflets available from the Edenbridge Information Centre.

Pathway through Emmetts Garden

EMMETTS GARDEN (NT) C-1 A lovely five-acre hillside garden in the care of the National Trust since 1964. Its laying-out in the late 19th century was much influenced by designer William Robinson and it contains many rare trees and shrubs from various parts of the world. There are rose and rock gardens and spectacular views over the Eden Valley. *Tea Room, Shop (Tel: 01732 751 509)*. Emmetts is on our **Walk 6**.

FORDCOMBE D-4 Most of the houses of this mid-19th-century estate village are attractively sited around a small sloping green. The church, completed in 1848, has a small bellcote and stands well below the green. On the opposite side of the road to both church and green, the tile-hung Chafford Arms (*Tel: 01892 740 267*) has a restaurant and offers locally-brewed ales.

FOUR ELMS C-2 Centred upon a crossroads with large duckpond nearby, this modest village has an inn, the Four Elms (*Tel: 01732 700 460*) beside the road out towards Tunbridge Wells and not far beyond, stands Four Elms' elegant little Victorian church. This has a slender spire and neat apsidal west-end housing its baptistery. There are

Four Elms Church

a number of interesting features created by members of the Arts and Crafts Movement including a lovely reredos in glowing white, unpolished Torquay marble, representing the Adoration of the Magi. This was designed by the outstanding artist and architect, William Lethaby, who also designed the chancel screen. Other works of interest include glass in a window in the north transept inserted after the 39-45 War to replace glass destroyed by a V1 flying bomb which exploded on the cricket ground opposite*. Our **Walk 10** starts from the Four Elms Inn.

*This area, between London and the V1 launching sites in Northern France, witnessed many of these noisy and dangerous devices flying overhead and became known as Flying Bomb Alley. Some were brought down by wires suspended from barrage balloons and others were shot down by the RAF, but in almost every case they still exploded when hitting the ground and caused much damage. It was a mercy that the launching sites were soon overrun by advancing allied troops after the hard-fought breakout following the Normandy landings.

The Woodman Inn, Goathurst Common

GOATHURST COMMON D-1 The nearby Woodman Inn (*Tel: 01732 750 296*) lies on the route of our **Walk 5**, and is probably the best access point for richly wooded Goathurst Common.

GODDEN GREEN E-1 The attractive little Buck's Head Inn (*Tel: 01732 761 330*) looks out across its wide green with duckpond and it is from here that our **Walk 16** commences. Our **Walk 8** also passes through it.

GREENSAND WAY B-1 to F-1 This long-distance path follows the ridge of greensand rock across Surrey and Kent, to the edges of Romney Marsh, almost to the Kent coast. Its total length is 107 miles, a small section of which runs along the Greensand ridge in the area covered by this guide. Details are not provided here as Kent County Council provides these via its *Explore Kent* website, with a "chapter" covering the route between Westerham and Shipbourne. Several of our Walks follow sections of the Greensand Way.

HANGING BANK   C-1 This wooded escarpment is best reached from a car park at a small crossroads half-a-mile east of **Ide Hill**. There are paths starting from both sides of the car park leading along the top of the escarpment to viewpoints from where there are fine prospects of the High Weald and the sparkling waters of **Bough Beech Reservoir**. These paths are on the course of the **Greensand Way**, which can therefore be joined here. It also lies on the course of our **Walk 5**. Much of the area above Hanging Bank is known as Stubbs Wood.

HAYSDEN COUNTRY PARK E-3 The River Medway runs through this park, which also includes two lakes, Barden Lake and Haysden Water. Here will be found a wide variety of waterfowl, wild flowers, and insect life. The Straight Mile, which leads off the Medway, was dug as a canal in 1830, but neither this nor the Stone Lock linking the Straight Mile to the Medway were ever put into use. This attractive park can be reached from a car park at Lower Haysden, west of **Tonbridge**, and is also on the course of our **Walk 20**. Both the **Eden Valley Walk** and the **Tudor (cycle) Trail** also pass through it.

At Haysden Country Park

HEVER C-3 Small village at the gates of **Hever Castle**, with an inn of character, the King Henry VIII, with its unique sign, showing the monarch's front and back view (*Tel: 01732 862 457*).   The parish church opposite has a tall, slender spire on a 14th-century tower while inside will be found the substantial table tomb of Sir Thomas Bullen (*Boleyn*), father of Anne Boleyn, and thereby grandfather of our first great Queen Elizabeth.   This tomb is topped by a fine brass of Sir Thomas and on the floor of the chancel there is another equally splendid brass depicting Margaret Cheyne.   Our **Walk 11** starts at the King Henry VIII Inn,   The Greyhound Inn (*Tel: 01732 862 221*) is situated on a quiet road well to the south of Hever and is on the course of our **Walk 11**.

HEVER CASTLE C-3   In 1903, American millionaire, William Waldorf Astor purchased the largely derelict castle, which had

The King Henry VIII Inn, Hever

Hever Castle

once belonged to the Bullen (*Boleyn*) family. During the next ten years he undertook an ambitious rebuilding and restoration of the castle itself and the creation of a 'Tudor village' to which it was linked. Similar care was lavished on the surrounding grounds. The waters of the River Eden were diverted to flow into an excavated 40-acre lake and magnificent Italian-style gardens were created with genuine Greek and Roman sculptures purchased over a number of years. In the meantime William Waldorf had become a British citizen and in 1916 he was created Lord Astor. All the restoration work at Hever was carried out with great taste and imagination and it has been well maintained ever since. Both castle and grounds are open to the public and a visit here will be enhanced by the story of the castle's restoration and of the Astor family, who have contributed so much to British life. *Restaurant, Gift Shop and other visitor facilities. (Tel: 01732 865 224; www.hevercastle.co.uk)*

HILDENBOROUGH E-2 Situated to the north-west of Tonbridge, in the 18th century this village stood on one of Kent's earliest turnpike roads. This was much used by fashionable London visitors to Tunbridge Wells, but Hildenboough only grew significantly from the 1870s onwards, due largely to the coming of railway links to London. It is now almost a suburb of Tonbridge. Hildenborough's mid-19th-century church has a shingled spire and its windows include one designed by Edward Burne-Jones. The village has no fewer than three inns -the Half Moon (*Tel: 01732 832 390*), the Flying Dutchman *(Tel: 01732 834 450)*, the Cock Horse *(Tel: 01732 833 232)* and a hotel, Hilden Manor (*Tel: 01732 362 784*).

Should you wish to read about Hildenborough's experiences during World War II, *Wikipedia* has an article full of interest. This includes an account of a German airman who bailed out of his aircraft only to land on the roof of the Boiling Kettle Tearooms, where he was given tea and cakes until the arrival of a policeman. Life at Hildenborough was not all bad in those days!

IDE HILL C-1 Grouped around a wide sloping green this village has several pleasant old houses, an inn called the Cock (*Tel: 01732 750 310*) and a small Victorian church, reputed to be the highest in Kent. Approached beneath an attractive lychgate, the church dates only from 1865. The sanctuary within has a light and airy ceiling which was installed in memory of President Kennedy, who was assassinated in 1963. The east

Octavia Hill Memorial Bench, Ide Hill

window below it was only installed in 1947 to replace the original which had been destroyed by enemy action in the Second World War. Off to the right of the road leading up to the church a footpath, initially up a drive, leads to a dramatic viewpoint. To reach this, soon turn right, off the drive and then veer left to go along a path with horse paddock to its right and benches beside it. At the end of this path fork left in woodland and follow a Greensand Way waymark down through woodland to reach the Octavia Hill Memorial Bench, from which there are superb views out over the Weald. This commemorates Octavia Hill, one of the founders of the National Trust (see **Crockham Hill**). Our **Walks 5 and 6** both start from Ide Hill's Cock Inn.

IGHTHAM MOTE (NT) F-1
Standing in a secluded valley, this is a beautifully- restored medieval moated manor house with later additions. The moat of clear spring water is graced by swans and full of fish. See especially the lovely courtyard, the Great Hall, and the crypt. It is also possible to see the private apartments of Charles Henry Robinson, who gave Ightham Mote to the National Trust in 1985. There are gardens with water features, lakes and woodland

Ightham Mote

walks. *Restaurant, Shop.* (*Tel: 01732 810 378*). Our **Walk 4** passes very close to Ightham Mote and provides an excellent pedestrian access to it.

KNOLE (NT) D-1 Knole, one of the largest private houses in England, is set in more than 1,000 acres of magnificent deer park, through which there are several marked trails. It stands close to the old centre of **Sevenoaks**, with its unobtrusive entrance from the High Street close to the church. The present building was started in 1456 by Thomas Bourchier, Archbishop of Canterbury, and it was occupied by subsequent archbishops until Henry VIII filched it from Cranmer. After Henry's death and several changes of ownership it came into the hands of Queen Elizabeth. She gave it, complete with sitting tenant, to her cousin, Thomas Sackville. He took full possession in 1603 and it remained in his family until 1946 when the 4th Lord Sackville presented it to the National Trust. Our **Walk 16** passes by Knole on its way through Knole's magnificent parkland.

Knole is a treasure-house of Jacobean furniture and textiles and its great staterooms are full of Sackville portraits. The delightful Orangery should not be

Knole

68

missed, nor attics and tower rooms, which have now been opened up. The Hidden History Exhibition in the former estate office features people's memories of visiting, living and working at Knole and reminds us that this great house was the early home of Vita Sackville-West and the inspiration for her novel, *Orlando*. *Visitor Centre, Shop, Tea-room. (Tel: 01732 462 100).*

LEIGH E-3 This village's large green incorporates a cricket ground and is surrounded by trim houses and cottages. Most of these were estate houses built by the prosperous owners of nearby Hall Place, a large Elizabethan mansion, largely rebuilt in the mid-19th century following a disastrous fire. The green is also overlooked by a church dating from the 13th century but heavily restored in the 19th. Happily the restorers spared the 14th-century painted glass depicting the Virgin Mary in the top light in the north aisle window. Do not overlook the impressive 15th-century font. Our **Walk 14** starts from the Fleur de Lis Inn (*Tel: 01732 832 235*) in this village and it is also on the course of our **Walk 20**.

War Memorial at Leigh

LONDON TO LEWES WAY (See Roman Road)

MARKBEECH C-4 There are splendid views southwards over the Weald from this small village set on high ground, beneath which runs a deep and still busy railway tunnel. Apart from a small Victorian church, Markbeech has only a few houses and cottages and an inn, the Kentish Horse (*Tel: 01342 850 493*). Most of the cottages date back to the mid-19th century and were built by the Chetwyn-Talbots of the nearby Falconhurst Estate. The church contains several Talbot monuments and has a very pleasant luminous interior. The well-known Falconhurst Cricket Club has a tree-bordered cricket field with an attractive pavilion. *Markbeech -The Unknown Village* by Timothy Boyle (1999) gives a detailed history of the village. Our **Walk 15** starts from Markbeech and it is also on the course of our **Walk 11**.

MARSH GREEN B-3 In years past Marsh Green had an inn, four shops, a tea-room, and a cobbler. Today only the inn survives - the welcoming tile-hung Wheatsheaf (*Tel: 01732 864 091*). The tall-spired Victorian church looks out over a wide tree-bordered green. This is said to have been, in 1886, the anticipated venue for the last bare-knuckle fight in England. Due to fear of possible police intervention, the fight was moved to London and Marsh

The Wheatsheaf Inn, Marsh Green

Green thereby lost any chance of lasting fame. This village is on the course of the Edenbridge Boundary Walk (South Section). This is about six-and-a-half miles in length. There is also a circular walk starting from Marsh Green which is either two or four miles in length. Both of these walks are described in free leaflets obtainable either from the Edenbridge Information Centre or the adjoining Museum. Our **Walk 18** also passes through Marsh Green.

MEDWAY, RIVER E-3 etc Rising in the Sussex High Weald, this river is about seventy miles in length. It flows into our area just to the south-west of **Fordcombe** and it is soon joined by the more modest River Eden near **Penshurst**. It flows out of our area to the east of **Tonbridge**, on its way to the Thames Estuary at Sheerness. This river is navigable upstream as far as **Tonbridge** although attempts were made in the 19th century to extend this to **Leigh**. **The Eden Valley Walk** follows parts of its course from **Penshurst** to **Tonbridge**. Cyclists on the **Tudor Trail** will also keep within sight of the Medway during most of their journey between Tonbridge Castle and Penshurst.

ONE TREE HILL (NT) E-1 Here is a network of paths extending from a car park on a minor road to the east of Knole Park. These paths include the **Greensand Way** and our **Walks 9 and 16**. There are fine views from an open area looking southwards over the Weald. Bluebells are also much in evidence here in springtime.

The view southwards from One Tree Hill

PENSHURST D-3 Set in lovely wooded country, Penshurst has many medieval, Tudor and later buildings, the best of which are the group of timber-framed 15th-century houses on either side of the gateway to the church. Parts of the latter date from around 1200, but the interior of this church was extensively altered in the 1850s by Sir George Gilbert Scott. The Sidney Chapel is filled with memorials to the Sidney family of **Penshurst Place** including a white marble monument to Sir Robert Sidney and nine of his children. The Leicester Arms Hotel (*Tel: 01892 871 617*) stands at the centre of the village, not far from the church and marks the start of our **Walks 17 and 20**. Penshurst is also on the course of the **Eden Valley Walk** and at the western end of the **Tudor (cycle) Trail**.

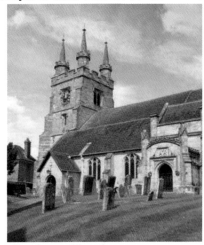

PENSHURST PLACE D-3 Constructed of local sandstone and mellow Tudor brick, this splendid building has a magnificently-proportioned 14th-century Great Hall, with the rest dating from the 16th century or later. It has belonged to the Sidney family since the reign of Edward VI and their most famous member, the poet and courtier, Sir Philip Sidney, was born here in 1559. More recently, after Penshurst suffered damage during the

Penshurst Church

Second World War, a direct descendant, William Sidney, who later became 1st Viscount De L'Isle and the last English Governor-General of Australia, inherited Penshurst. He moved into Penshurst Place in 1946, and brought the house and the gardens back to their former glory. His son, the current

Penshurst Place

owner, Philip Sidney, 2nd Viscount De L'Isle continues his family's stewardship with Pemshurst retaining the warmth and character of a much-loved family home.. There is much to interest including the house with its fine state rooms, portraits and furniture. See also the lovely gardens, and the park, with nature trails and adventure playground for young visitors. *Restaurant, Cafe, Gift Shop (Tel: 01892 870 307)*.

Quebec House, Westerham

QUEBEC HOUSE (NT) B-1 *Situated in* **Westerham** *near the point where the B2026, Edenbridge Road joins the A25,* this elegant Georgian house was the boyhood home of General Wolfe. He was best known for his dramatic victory at Quebec in 1759 and his tragic death on its battlefield. There is a most interesting exhibition covering Wolfe's life and death, and the military campaign in which he was involved. The house is furnished as it would have been in the days of Wolfe's childhood and is full of 18th-century flavour. The National Trust invites visitors to "try their hands at the pastimes Wolfe's family would have enjoyed and to take a cup of tea in Mrs Wolfe's charming garden. *Tearoom. Shop. (Tel: 01732 868 381)*.

RIVER EDEN (See Eden, River)

RIVER MEDWAY (See Medway, River)

ROMAN ROAD Now known as the London to Lewes Way, this Roman road ran for 44 miles, from the Watling Street in Peckham, to the South Downs just to the east of Lewes. It is overlaid by a modern road in only one place, this being **Edenbridge's** long High Street. Its course continues on the same alignment at least as far as Ashdown Forest. There were extensive iron workings in the wealden country in Roman times and the resulting slag was often used for surfacing the road. This material has provided archaeologists with vital evidence of the road's course. For further details, read I D Margary's *Roman Roads in the Weald*, which has detailed, large-scale strip maps showing the road's course through the area.

SEVENOAKS D-1 Although Sevenoaks has long been the home of many commuters to London, and has grown in size accordingly, it still retains much of the character of a country town. There are many 16th-, 17th- and 18th-century houses in the older part of the town together with Sevenoaks School which was founded in 1418 and which is thereby the third oldest non-denominational school in the country. The school now occupies Georgian buildings

One of Sevenoaks' attractive little shopping streets

of grey ragstone. The Parish Church has a 14th-century tower, the rest being largely 15th-century with later restoration. Do not miss a visit to the interesting Sevenoaks Museum in Buckhurst Lane. This is part of 'Sevenoaks Kaleidoscope' (together with the Library and Art Gallery). For magnificent **Knole**, see separate entry.

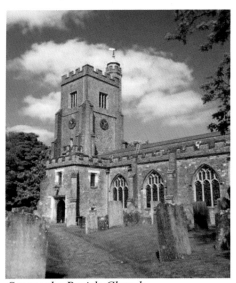

Sevenoaks Parish Church

SEVENOAKS WILDLIFE RESERVE D-1 - Just to the north of our map. Situated to the north of Sevenoaks and just to the north of the A25, the extensive Sevenoaks Wildlife Reserve is well worth visiting. It has a mixed habitat of ponds, seasonally flooded pools, reed beds, and woodland and a wide variety of birds can be found here. *Tea bar serving hot and cold drinks, snacks and ice-creams, Gift Shop, Visitor Centre. (Tel: 01732 456 407).*

SEVENOAKS WEALD D-2 Situated beneath the slopes of the Greensand ridge and well to the south of Sevenoaks, this village was once known simply as Weald. It became a separate parish in 1861. The attractively-signed Windmill Inn *(Tel: 01732 463 330)* stands near the centre of the village, on the edge of a wide village green and marks the start of our **Walk 19**. The little Parish Church, which dates from 1821, stands on high ground at the northern end of the village. Although reduced in height in the 1890s, the church's 1870 tower still stands proud, and looks convincingly medieval. The interior, with its small west balcony, is pleasingly warm in feeling and the elaborate chancel ceiling is painted with emblems of the Passion.

The medieval, timber-framed house, Long Barn, at the far end of Long Barn Road was the first home of Sir Harold Nicholson and his wife Vita Sackville-West from 1915 until 1930, before they moved to Sissinghurst. Standing in a garden designed by Lutyens it is very much a private house and should not be intruded upon. Distant glimpses may be obtained from the early course of our **Walk 19**. The poet Edward Thomas, who was killed in action in 1917, lived for a time at nearby Else's Farm.

SHIPBOURNE F-1 Lying in wooded country beneath the Greensand ridge, this scattered village (pronounced 'Shibbun') is centred on a large green, or common. The lively Chaser Inn (Tel: 01732 810 360) looks across to the common, its name reminding us that many winning horses were trained here over the years, including those belonging to the late Queen Mother. The training stables, run by Major Peter Cazalet, were part of the Fairlawne Estate, which until recent times was owned by the Cazalet family. The contents of the stout-towered Victorian church include an impressive 18th-century wall monument to Lord and Lady Barnard, owners of Fairlawne well before the Cazalets. Our **Walk 4** starts from the Chaser Inn.

SMARTS HILL D-4 A scattered hamlet in wooded country about two miles south of Penshurst with two outstanding inns situated not far from each other: the Spotted Dog (Tel: 01892 870 253), from which there are splendid views over the Medway valley, and the Bottle House (Tel: 01892 870 306). Our **Walk 2** starts from the Spotted Dog and, in its closing stages, also passes close by the Bottle House.

The Bottle House Inn, Smarts Hill

SOUTHBOROUGH F-4 This is labelled "South", as it was once the southern part of Tonbridge, but it is now a suburban extension of Tunbridge Wells. It has a large green, where cricket has been played for over 200 years, and three churches, two built in the 19th century and one in the early 20th. There were iron forges here in the 16th century and although these were closed by the mid-18th century, at least one was taken over for the manufacture of gunpowder. Although this mill blew up soon after it opened, it is still remembered by a road called Powder Mill Lane. Hotels and inns here include the Imperial (Tel: 01892 514 135), the Weavers (Tel: 01892 529 896), the Hand & Sceptre (Tel: 01892 529 292) and the Crown (Tel: 01892 524 993).

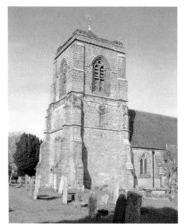

Speldhurst Church

SPELDHURST E-4 A pleasant village, poised on a hill slope above the Medway Valley. Its medieval church was burnt down in 1791, having been struck by lightning, and the present Victorian church replaced a second, short-lived building in 1870. The present church, with its lofty interior, has an unusually attractive series of stained glass windows, most of which were made by Morris and Co, the workshop of William Morris, and some of which are based on the designs of Edward Burne-Jones. Read about these windows in the interesting booklet on sale in the church. If you have access to the Web do look for The Mice of St Mary's --- and remember - *"Just because you can't see them it doesn't mean they aren't there!"* There are a number of interesting tombstones in the churchyard, many of which pre-date the present church. The richly-timbered George and Dragon Inn is just below the church and interestingly aims to source all its ingredients (within reason!) from within a thirty-mile radius *(Tel: 01892 863125)*. A member of the Powell family, Lords of the Manor, the Rev. Baden Powell, was once vicar here, and was the father of Lord Baden-Powell, the founder of the Scout Movement.

SQUERRYES COURT B-1 Situated to the south side of the A25 at the western end of **Westerham**, this mellow-brick William and Mary manor house has been the home of the Warde family since 1731. The Wardes were friends of James Wolfe, the hero of Quebec, and it was here that he was handed his first commission. Squerryes Court is no longer open to the public.

STAFFHURST WOOD A-2 Owned in part by the Woodland Trust and also managed in part by Surrey Wildlife Trust, this extensive area of woodland is comprised largely of oak, ash and beech. It is crossed by a number of paths, including four public footpaths. It was once part of a royal hunting forest and during the Second World War was used as an ammunition dump in the months leading up to D Day. The Royal Oak Inn, on Caterfield Lane, situated just to its west, is well placed to cater for woodland walkers *(Tel: 01883 722 207)*. Our **Walk 3** starts from here before entering the wood.

A hint of bluebells in Staffhurst Wood

South Doorway, Stone Street Church

STONE STREET E-1 This scattered settlement below a long wooded ridge has two welcoming inns, the Snail Pub and Restaurant *(Tel: 01732 810 233)* and the Padwell Arms *(Tel: 01732 761 532)*, the latter marking the start of our **Walk 8**. The church stands on the edge of woodland well above both inns and just off the course of **Walk 8.** Dedicated to St Lawrence, it is named after the Parish of St Lawrence in the Isle of Wight. It was here that Rachel, the six-year-old daughter of the local landowners, died while on holiday and they built the church in her memory. It was completed in 1868 and Rachel's body was then re-buried in the churchyard. There is a picture of Rachel in one of the chancel windows.

STUBBS WOOD C-1 (See Hanging Bank)

SUSSEX BORDER PATH This long-distance path follows the inland boundary of the county of Sussex and is almost 150 miles in length. It was established as long ago as 1983 and its waymarking now appears to be rather sporadic on the length used by our **Walk 15**. Other sections have not been checked.

TONBRIDGE F-3 Until 1870, the town's name was spelt Tunbridge and today it is still pronounced *Tun-*, rather than *Ton-*. Since the Middle Ages it had been a prosperous market town and its prosperity grew further when, in 1740, the Medway became navigable. Today it has some light industry and it is surrounded by the homes of many London commuters. The Medway still flows through the town centre and on its banks are riverside walks and playing fields. On a mound just west of the High

Tonbridge Castle

Street are the impressive remains of a moated castle - a 13th-century gatehouse attached to an 18th-century building used as municipal offices. The castle is on the route of our **Walk 20**. There are some attractive old buildings in the little streets near the castle and in the northern part of the High Street. The well-known Tonbridge School was founded in 1553 although most of its present buildings are, like so many public schools, largely Victorian Gothic. The Parish Church has a stout 13th-century

Houses near the church, Tonbridge

tower and an impressively large interior with a Norman chancel arch and a fine east window. Inns in Tonbridge include the Stag's Head, with its fascinating collection of clocks (*Tel: 01732 352 017*), the Vauxhall (*Tel: 01732 773 111*), the New Drum (*Tel: 01732 773 291*), the tile-hung Ivy House (*Tel: 01771 249 382*), the supposedly haunted Cardinal's Error (*Tel: 01732 770 107*), and the Punch and Judy (*Tel: 01732 352 368*).

TOYS HILL C-1 A hamlet on the steep slopes of the Greensand ridge along a quiet terrace road known as Puddledock Lane. There was an inn here once, the Tally Ho, but this is now only a distant memory. There are splendid views out over the Weald towards Ashurst Forest and the South Downs from a National Trust seat beside a restored well-head. A short distance to its east there is a small triangular green

View from bench by the well-head, Toys Hill

overlooked by a stoutly-buttressed building dated 1910. From here there is a steep path climbing up into the Toys Hill Woods where there is a car park. There are over 200 acres of woodland which was one of several inspirations that prompted Octavia Hill to found the National Trust and which are now owned by the Trust. In the words of the Trust - *"It is a marvellous place to enjoy a peaceful, relaxing walk, admire fine views over the Weald and to discover the wildlife it supports."* There are waymarked walks from the car park and these are described on a notice board there and also on a most useful leaflet which is usually obtainable from a dispenser at the same point. Both the Red and the Green Walks take walkers past the site of **Weardale Manor** (*see* separate entry). Use the leaflet to locate paths close to the Fox and Hounds Inn (*Tel: 01732 750 328*), which is on the road a short distance north of the car park. This inn is also close to the course of our **Walk 6**, which also passes through the car park and the Weardale Manor site. Also usually obtainable from the same dispenser is a leaflet describing the Octavia Hill Centenary Trail - two separate walks (*both of which start from the well-head at Toys Hill, but don't try to park there*) making up a figure of eight. Octavia Hill Walk 1 is 4 miles long and passes Octavia Hill's commemorative seat at **Ide Hill**, before returning past **Emmetts Garden**. Octavia Hill Walk 2 is 6 miles long and passes through **Crockham Hill**, Octavia's burial place, the hamlets of Froghole and French Street with an optional stop at **Chartwell**.

TUDELEY F-3   Small village with a simple medieval church, largely rebuilt in the 18th-century. This is down a lane by a farm and has a set of unique stained glass windows, all designed by the highly-talented Russian-born artist, Marc Chagall. The East window, a breathtaking riot of lovely blues, was commissioned by the parents of Sarah D'Avigdor-Goldsmid, in memory of their daughter, who died in a sailing accident in 1963. The remaining windows were added in the years following, the last being completed in 1985, the year of Chagall's death. Any visitor here cannot fail to be deeply moved. These windows are described in detail in a leaflet available in the church. There is a welcoming inn nearby, the Poacher (*Tel: 01732 358 934*).

East Window, Tudeley Church

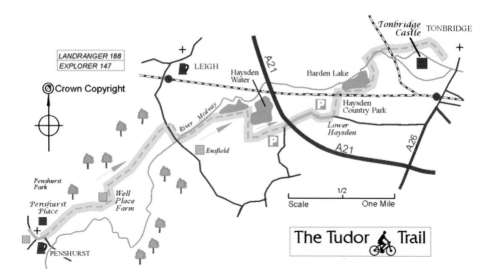

TUDOR (CYCLE) TRAIL, THE

This six-mile trail runs from Tonbridge Castle to Penshurst Place and much of it is used by our **Walk 20**. For further information see *www.kent.gov.uk/explorekent*

TUNBRIDGE WELLS F-4

At some time in the year 1606 Lord North, while travelling the area, came upon a chalybeate spring, the waters of which soon acquired a reputation for health-giving. Lord North claimed that the waters cured his consumption and in no time, Tunbridge Wells became a fashionable destination for the nobility. 'The Wells' remained in fashion for at least two hundred years. At one

Spring sunshine at the Pantiles, Tunbridge Wells

time the noted Beau Nash came from Bath as Master of Ceremonies and Thackeray, who lived in a small house on the Common, used it as the background for two of his novels. The spring that brought fame to Tunbridge is still not forgotten and in summer it is possible to sample the cool chalybeate spring water at its present source in the north-west corner of the Pantiles (*see below*).

Facing the large triangular Common close to the town centre are many fine Georgian and early-Victorian buildings. The famous Pantiles is a paved and terraced pedestrian precinct which was the fashionable centre of the Wells in Regency times. It has a curving row of colonnaded shops faced by a line of lime trees and is particularly

The Chalybeate Spring, Tunbridge Wells

beautiful in spring when the limes are in fresh leaf. Tunbridge Wells Museum and Art Gallery (*Tel: 01892 554 171*) is to be found in the Civic Centre at Mount Pleasant and contains the largest collection of Tunbridge Ware; this being a distinctive style of decorative marquetry woodware which was made in Tunbridge Wells between the late 1600s and the 1920s. It also has outstanding collections of dolls, toys and games and holds special exhibitions regularly. Dunorlan Park, a little way out of town, on the A264, has wide grassy slopes and fine views to the Weald. There is also a boating lake and cafe, and boats can be hired from two weeks before Easter until the end of October. The Spa Valley Railway (*Tel: 01892 537 715*) is a steam and diesel heritage line running between Tunbridge Wells West Station and Eridge (off our map). Tunbridge Wells West Station is adjacent to Sainsbury's supermarket at Nevil Terrace. The engine shed here was built in 1886 and is a unique survivor from the age of steam. It now houses a collection of historic locomotives and carriages. At High Rocks (*Tel: 01892 515 532*), about two miles west of the town centre, there are many impressive sandstone rocks interlinked by eleven bridges, providing a scenic walk in delightful woodlands. There are also many opportunities for rock-climbing. There is also a station on the Spa Valley Railway here (*see above*).

UNDERRIVER   E-1

Minute and very attractive village beneath the woodlands in the vicinity of **One Tree Hill** with a small Victorian church. Its simple, lofty interior is well lit by many clear glass windows. It was designed by George Gilbert Scott, perhaps best known for his designs of St Pancras Station and the Albert Memorial. Close by is the White Rock Inn (*Tel: 01732 833 112*). This very traditional inn has

The White Rock Inn, Underriver

its own petanque pitch and it is also possible to play the old-fashioned Kentish pub game of Bat and Trap here. This village's name, "Underriver" is derived from the Old English *le ryver* which translates into modern English as "under the hill". Our **Walk 9** starts from the White Rock Inn.

WEALDEN ROUND, THE

This 50-mile route around the area covered by this guidebook is in course of development and a guidebook to it should be available at some time in 2015. If tackled all in one go, this will present quite a challenge and all those who complete it will receive a certificate of congratulations and thanks from the Hospice in the Weald. It is hoped that walkers taking up this challenge will possibly obtain sponsorship support from friends, relations and work

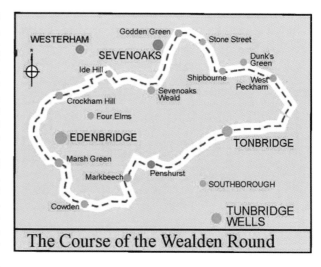

The Course of the Wealden Round

colleagues, thus raising funds for this vitally important charity. More details available from the Hospice in the Weald on 01892 820 586 - speaking to Sara Clark.

View westwards from the site of Weardale Manor

WEARDALE MANOR, SITE OF B-1 This site can be easily reached from the **Toys Hill** car park. There are splendid views across the counties of Kent, East and West Sussex and Surrey from the level terrace where Weardale Manor once stood. This massive house was built by Lord Weardale as a summer country retreat and was completed in 1906. Lord Weardale died in 1923 and his widow, finding the house too lonely, decided to live permanently in London. She died in 1934 and her nephew, who inherited Weardale Manor, allowed it to fall into a state of disrepair. It was finally demolished in 1939, the process being completed by two bombs that fell on the ruins during the 39-45 War. There is a lonely memorial at the rear of the manor site, to two Robinson brothers killed in the First World War. Not far behind, in the woods above the manor site are the remains of its castellated water supply tank, now utilised by the National Trust as a hibernation site for bats. Our **Walk 6** passes by this very pleasant area.

WESTERHAM B-1 Lying below wooded Westerham Hill, the highest point in Kent, Westerham has many timbered and mellow-brick buildings and still has the flavour of a small market town. Despite relief by the M25, the A25 continues to provide Westerham with overmuch through-traffic. It has two especially interesting houses, **Quebec House** at its eastern end and **Squerryes Court** at its western end. Both have connections with General James Wolfe, although only the former is open to the public. There is a good car park at the eastern end of the town and it is possible to walk from there to **Quebec House** and then on to the church. This stands above a

Sir Winston Churchill, on the green at Westerham

sloping churchyard, a wide, much-restored building, with both north and south aisles as long as its nave. Beyond the church there is a sloping triangular green on which there are two statues, one of General Wolfe and the other of Sir Winston Churchill. The latter is the work of the outstanding sculptor, Oscar Nemon and was cast from the same mould as that of the rather better-known statue in Parliament Square. The Market Square is beyond the green and is edged by a number of attractive shops and inns including the King's Arms Hotel (*Tel: 01959 562 990*) which stands at the start of our **Walk 12**. Other inns include the Grasshopper (*Tel: 01959 563 136*) and the George and Dragon (*Tel: 01959 563 071*).

Houses overlooking the green at Westerham